Hardscrabble

THE

POETRY
SERIES

Hardscrabble

POEMS BY KEVIN MCFADDEN

The University of Georgia Press   Athens and London

Published by The University of Georgia Press
Athens, Georgia 30602
© 2008 by Kevin McFadden
All rights reserved
Set in Minion Pro
by Graphic Composition, Inc., Bogart, Georgia
Printed and bound by Thomson-Shore
The paper in this book meets the guidelines for
permanence and durability of the Committee on
Production Guidelines for Book Longevity of the
Council on Library Resources.

Printed in the United States of America

12   11   10   09   08   P   5   4   3   2   1

Library of Congress Cataloging-in-Publication Data

McFadden, Kevin.
Hardscrabble : poems / by Kevin McFadden.
      p.   cm. — (The VQR poetry series)
ISBN-13: 978-0-8203-3118-8 (pbk. : alk. paper)
ISBN-10: 0-8203-3118-X (pbk. : alk. paper)
I. Title.
PS3613.C437H37 2008
811'.6—dc22   2007045062

British Library Cataloging-in-Publication Data available

"We were, of course, never as innocent as we pretended to be, even as a child is not as innocent as is implied in the use of the child as a symbol of innocency."

—Reinhold Niebuhr, *The Irony of American History*

Contents

Acknowledgments

Grateful acknowledgments are made to the following journals for first publishing poems that appear in this collection:

The Antioch Review: a section from "Famed Cities" ("Tomfoolery, Seventeen")

Archipelago.org: a section from "Famed Cities" ("Loan, Glasgow"), "Diet Meats," and "Test of Merit"

Blackbird: "Feet"

Chicago Review: "It Has an I"

Denver Quarterly: "Is," "It's Smut," and "Authentic"

Drunken Boat: sections from "Famed Cities" ("Dread, Phalanx") and "Time" ("Decimation, Tenth Legion")

Greensboro Review: "Ears"

Hotel Amerika: "A Dance Theater of Mutts"

Massachusetts Review: a section from "Time" ("Mode, Edom")

Parnassus: "The Faucet"

Pleiades: "Die Satan!"

Ploughshares: "Hate"

Poetry: "It's a Cue, the Name," "A Tone Deficit," "Meta-Forest," and three sections from "Time" ("Room, Ottoman," "Campfire, Lignum," and "Dubious, Water View")

Potomac Review: "Media" and "Court Seated"

Prairie Schooner: two sections from "Time" ("Credit, Check" and "Correspondence, Natural Bridge")

Quarterly West: "Meditate Sea to Sea" and "It's Tarmac"

Seneca Review: "Drift"

Shenandoah: two sections from "Time" ("New Dominion, Charlottes-ville" and "Soldiers, Appomattox")

Smartish Pace: "A French Statue," selected winner of the 2006 Erskine J. Poetry Prize

Streetlight: "Statue" and two sections from "Time" ("Library, Alexandria" and "Times Dispatch, Richmond")

Verse: "I.e."

"The Faucet," "Room, Ottoman," "Campfire, Lignum," "Dubious, Water View," and "Tomfoolery, Seventeen" were reprinted online by *Poetry Daily* (www.poems.com).

I would like to thank my teachers for their patience and care (the drafts they experienced give *me* chills): Br. Joseph Chvala (C.S.C.), Marilyn Throne, James Reiss, Rita Dove, Gregory Orr, and Charles Wright. Three cheers for Don Selby and Diane Boller of Poetry Daily; three more for Miami University and the invaluable support I received from the Goldman Memorial Prize. Gratitude to the poets who helped this book with advice, votes of confidence, careful reading, and close editing along the way: Heather McHugh, Kay Ryan, Ted Genoways, and most significantly Terence Huber. I count on my nuclear family's clean-burning, renewable resource of wisdom—whose warmth exceeds its degrees. Finally, my wife, formidable poet and Scrabble opponent, Angie Hogan.

Hardscrabble

Is

written this way
to almost resemble
                    us:
half-straight,
            half-sinuous.

A Dance Theater of Mutts

Call it what you will,

        Canis americanus,

what goes on all fours

        and in the neighbor's tulips.

(Diversion at work,

        such sleights of

and; here *go* is both

        "wander" and "piss.")

Here anything goes.

        I've wandered.

You're pissed.

        We leap for these rings:

canis is "dog" in Latin

        and "you sing."

        And you sing

of a land where
people pick up
after mutts. We

        —snap at the strange.
        —like shiny coats.
        —bring and get.
        —bury our bones.

Words don't mean
so much as tone.
We envy the dog,
it goes without

      saying. There
      it goes again.

———————

      It goes again

to show the leash

      has more than one end.

They've picked up
after us, after all.

      (Ever watch one lick up
      its own sick? It does.
      It's something to chew on.)

In this three-ring

      circus I must beg you

to call a poem, call it
Killer, call it Cuddles:

      we call it home.

Call it what you will.

I.e.

Lo, it's her lethargic
hello, it's her tragic
height or cellar. It's
her agile torch's lit
oracle. It's her light.
It's her locale, right?
It charts her oil, gel
lather, her logic, its
chi. Its legal rhetor-
ic a lighter holster,
its collar tree-high.
Its relic hearth-log
heritage, rich tolls,
rich tollgate heirs.
It's grace or the hill.
It's the hill, ergo, car
roll. It's the rich age,
gosh, a little richer.
Go tell its hierarch
or healer its glitch:
it's a gothic hell, err-
or a tight chiseller.
It's right here, local
call to higher rites.
Go hither, its caller.
It coheres all right. . . .

A Hut of Cretins

Or think of the Great American Hovel:
log cabin that the town keeps on the common
or the one-room clapboard schoolhouse
it restores and pays to have swept on Tuesdays.
The three retirees who work for twenty-five
a week and take turns pulling the flag
up the rope each morning.

                                    How a nation
tends its notion of the mud even after the marble,
roughly imagined huts along the Tiber, Thames,
Potomac. One room: how like the mind
before its mansions, and how able to produce
at a glance the unwashed face, the brute
nose wiped with a sleeve while the labor
of refreshing inkwells is repeated or while mother
minds the kettle and the roof keeps leaking its
meaning into a bucket.

                                    And yet
the atrium, impluvium, and pillowed triclinium.
And yet the vestibule, the chamber, antechamber.
And yet the dome's delightful acoustical trick
which gives positioned listeners soft words clear
from the other side of the floor. And yet the Victorian
shorter-than-normal doors to seclude the servants.
And yet the dumbwaiter bricked into the hearth,
curiously and conveniently the width

of one wine bottle, dark hands hauling the rope
from the cellar at the signal.

One room:
how like the soul before its oldest and returned-to
hidden portals.

Meditate Sea to Sea

Let America be America again.
Ice-age ambiance. Later a mira-
cle air: a meat mania, ice-barge,
ice-amble. A tie. Agrarian came
later, Inca came, a bare image I
bear. An Eric came, agile at aim
(let America be a maniac, I rage).
Italian came—macabre, I agree.
Came Iberia, came Angle, a rat I
rate, a marine bilge. Came a CIA
angelic era, a tame iambic ear.
Bacteria came in a mire, algae
era. Militia came, began a race,
a crime, eager aim, Cain at Abel.
At Abe L. Imagine a ceramic era,
ceramic ear: I am it. A lab. A gene
I age. A meme trace. A bicranial
air age, a bicameral cinema, et
cetera, a manic beige malaria,
a carnage. America I let be. I am
a cameraman, I create a big lie
(let America be a camera I gain),
I am a cabaret emcee, a girl in a
bar, I am a teenage circle. I am a
Miami tribe, an eagle, a car, ace
airman. Elegiac America, a bet:
let America be a magic arena I
anagram. I bet I care (came a lie,
a clear image), I bet America an
animal acreage, I bet America

beer I can amalgamate air, ice-
berg. An ale. Ace-at-ear, I mimic a
man (bare me) I cite a racial age
(bear me) I glaciate Americana—
I'm a rain. Let America be a cage;
I remain a gate, a Mecca. I blare
Niagara, I accelerate, maim, be
a beam, I emanate a grail, Circe
mirage. America, a neat cable I
tie in. America, a gala embrace.
Let America be America: a gain.

Drift

Recalling the Murderers Bible, an 1801 edition in which Jude 16 reads "These are murderers" instead of "murmurers"

Float a moment. Let all go. Let all
sink. There are screams, live cargo in the holds
(they are horses, not men—though there were men)
going down,
        down,
            dying,
                dead. Detach

your head then get inside it. Sit quiet. Sit so still
it scares you how fast the continent can drift.

Fact is this: *We.*
        We are here.
                  We move
a little farther away from the Old World every year.
Foreign as the horse and so learned
               (belowdeck)
in murmurs emerged our tongue
             bit by bit

trained by rein or punch in the neck. Begins with

a mare
      in a sense
            (as in night? as in horse)

                 innocence
                         (as in Troy? as in plain horse-sense).
              It speaks to you.
                         It speaks in bucks, in the flying change
(sometimes I say *you* when I mean *me*)
can bruise when it kicks
                         it hurts you so to get
behind it. Pronounce "terror"
         as the English do (hear *terra*)
. . . o there we learned to love a land

and fear it.   There took the roll, took the *rogue*

out of Old World *progress* (our own frog-throated *progress*
still in progress) for all it's helped.

                         There took homes, took pride

in being so finally defined, our other alias
ELSE: and it
                         is its crafter's only promise
                                            a draft,
a drift.

A Hollywood Indian trick:
                         put your ear to the ground

to hear in your head what's coming.
                                   Close eyes
to the plain, hear *stampede*
                         or maybe *cavalry*
                                            or the word

you'd feel, whatever it was, which meant (in a sense)
catastrophe.

Put your ear to your tongue, our

                                                         tongue

(it is tied to your throat) and hear

what's being said beneath our breath. Else

drift
        and listen
                    tooth to tongue
                                   bit by bit.
And know if you won't listen:
                              what land, what language becomes us

                                          becomes us

whether or not we bend to hear it. . . .

It's a Cue, the Name

America a legible cue, low whinny.
America wan, ignoble clue—why lie?—
America yawning blue coil, wheel-
way lenience. America how'll I bug
lacy web? America how'll I genuine-
ly begin, cue American awe, how'll I
howl? Glibly. Ai, ai. McNuance ere we
libel an ugly American woe. I chew
a cigar. Hell (i.e. Columbine) we yawn.
America blew Waco in line, hugely.
America why callow ingenue bile?
America why beige oilcan, unwell
elegy, Hebraic wail, mine own caul?
America we bully alien, weigh con.
A malice binge, when will you care?

America when will you be angelic?
America bluely hewn logician, we
wince. America why Eagle bullion—
well America, Inc? Hyena guile, bow-
wow, canine gullible. Hey America
when will you balance CIA regime?
when will you be eager in acclaim?
America why ebullience, a glow in
lieu? We won America bellyaching.
Icy acre, a mule, Winnebago hill we
wheel away. Mingle a ribonucleic
law, become allegiance. I ruin. Why
when a micron away? Illegible cue,
concealable name we hug wirily. I
(we) be America: wily hallucinogen.

Famed Cities

I. OHIO WELCOMES YOU!

Enter in Unity, exit by Empire. Begin in Youngstown,
leave by Antiquity. New Paris, Delhi, Moscow, Venice—
the infamous river ins and landish outs.
Utopia's found on a map of Ohio, dream-keeping
a border. Alpha, yes, and yes again, Omega.
Shadyside, Lightsville, Torch and Brilliant.
I grew up near Mesopotamia, the Erie and the Ohio
were my Tigris and Euphrates.
The roads to Roads are worn back and forth,
Long Bottom, Ft. Recovery's quiet stretch around
Pt. Pleasant. And right outside of Friendship—
still, not awful close—you might try as others do
to make it to Delightful by nightfall.
Constitution, Pioneer, New Hope. . . .

II. PROMISE, ROOTSTOWN

I'll tell you what you need to know about me:
I never slept on any Parnassian ledges,
place names were always better than the places,
and somewhere, under that gunmetal sky
of childhood, one I loved died in my arms.
That's it. Anything else is embellishment.
I'll tell you what you need to know about me:
we won't be helped by swapping hard-knocks,
aside I've lain that *my pa can beat your pa* urge
to say *my pain can beat your pain.* I'll tell you what:
instead, from your far city, look around you,
it's all right there . . . the roots of longing and despair
in any order of cities . . . we have this between us.
I'll tell you what you need to know about me.

III. PROPHET, RICHFIELD

The night before I was born—I dug this out of
old papers—Muhammad Ali fought in the Coliseum.
I was looking for a star, I confess; nothing less
than the celestial to mark my stepping into the ring.
(We call it a ring, but somehow it's squared.) That night,
just south of soon-to-be-me, Muhammad fought in Richfield—
somewhere between, no kidding, Medina and Mecca.
The Coliseum's gone. Not Ali. He told the press all week
how he'd whip Wepner. And did. In fifteen.
(Already he'd gone dancin' with Johannson, stunned Liston.)
The star retreated. An unknown heavyweight emerged
ten-pounds-one-ounce the next day—no one blinked.
Give the newkid a shot (it was never prophesied) *he'll jab
and weave through anyone.* Messy, but in fourteen.

IV. LUCK, BRUNSWICK

Ah, for the suburbs' kids-can-play-in streets.
I was two when we moved. Farms nearby, some
charm. My family went for meaningless quirks,
so it probably didn't hurt that the Police Chief then
was a man named Crook. (Fire Chief? Burns.)
In school we read that settlers drew the name from a hat;
Brunswick turned up by democratic dumb luck—
maybe that's where its share ran out. Today all malls
or developments where forests stood, if they could
chop the tree off the city seal, someone would.
My friends I teased about the *leave* in Cleveland;
they teased back Brunswick's *run*. Home not,
as the saying goes, a place to hang your hat—
home where the hat, by name, by chance, hangs you.

V. SPEECH, LOGAN

Changed we were when this piece reached us;
my family was scribal, a tribal sub-caste of
the mighty Nacirema, grooming with care the next
come-of-age son for a local oratorical rite of spring
father had swept four years straight in his day.
We took it apart at each comma's little trigger,
cleaned it, loaded cold comforts into our muzzles
til Chief Logan's vengeance was glutted again —
that last, tongue-gulped disgust — *Not one.*
Reports could stir the blood, but who was left to mourn
for Logan? Our tough-luck savage saint, patron of
the too-trusting, whose all but unpronounceable real name
could not be confused with *Anglo*. All the same,
we came around spraying Logan, and they noticed.

VI. TOMFOOLERY, SEVENTEEN

Too shy for girls, yet there they were,
and too old for everything in my *Boys' Life*
save the jokepage and its dry Tom Swifties.
"Room for more than one," Tom said, *fortuitously.*
"No bruises," said Tom, *unabashed.*
Desire I had, confirmed, but low vocabulary.
Also a burn my Confirmation never cured —
"Some you lose," Tom said, *winsomely* —
the urge to be promiscuous. Til then, words.
Pent already, what could a boy repent?
I waited but I wanted, Swiftie-esque, I wanted
to be *titillated, pusillanimous,* and *indicative.*
For Lent I gave up Easter ever after,
which Tom forwent, relentlessly.

VII. CLERK, OXFORD

The code in Oxford, Ohio, has structures build up
no more than four levels. A notebook, college-ruled.
Scripsit: ledger begat literature. Talent. Interest.
Scripsit: play attention. Elsewhere, and in earnest:
"Did Freud forget what women want was one word
out of Chaucer?" God does not play dice, Dr. E,
he plays paradise. (Mr. E?) (Master E?)
$E = mc^2$, circled. The volta a turn for the verse.
Underlined: *If wommen hadde writen stories*
As clerkes han withinne hire oratories
They wolde han writen of men moore wikkednesse
Than al the mark of Adam may redresse.
That *mark of Cain?* is mine, miniscule, marginal.
My bank was Society, more tellers than stories.

VIII. BROTHERS, DAYTON

Guy-talk has a low, universal brogue, some tones
more local than others. ("You datin' a girl from Eaton
or eatin' a girl from Dayton?") Some are for
the buddies at school and some are just
between brothers. ("Sluts will sleep with anyone—
bitches sleep with anyone *but you.*")
The central metaphor for getting any
gettin-any gossip is flight, no question—
"I got shot down," "Aw man, I crashed and burned"—
the whole pilot idiom Ohio's by Wrights.
That buzz you barely make out over the drone?
An aviator's code of collusion; words that smirk,
beg the stewardesses to sit, prepare for a take-off.
We grew up in a kind of a cockpit.

IX. REPETITION, ROME

All roads lead to Rome. *And sewers,* adds Lowell.
And I to that, *Its plumbing led to lead.*
Ohio has four Romes, a lot to own—
but one of them had the sense to start
New. What else is? Well, we finally got our
McDonald's (you know you're backwoods when
fast food won't come to you) and soon that means
we can expect the rest competing for our obesity,
Kings and Queens and arches flung to the rustics.
Step by step they were led to decadent pleasures:
the lounge, the bath, the flashy banquet; these they called
in their ignorance civilization; just part of their servitude. . . .
Trickling through Tacitus, death, the first Roman
freedom: spreading in water, flowing in chains.

X. DREAD, PHALANX

ROMAN CANDLES O LATER ON BUST SKIES SHOOT OFF
UNFERAL OWLS HOOT IN GLOWING NOBLE NESTS NOW
TENSE TO GO JULY FOURTH ONE WITH EVERYTHING
SHADOW IN GLARES IMAGES IN THE IRREGARDING BAT
BRIGHT DARK BLING BLING YOUR OL LEGIRONS HAVENT
CEASED EVER HAVE THEY MASTER ROMANA HAVE
THEM JUST TINGLES SO THINKING OVER RANTING
BLEST ONGUENT O DAYTIME SUN STREAMS OVER A
CITY O JANUS FACED MUSA STOP PLAYING WITH
FIRE EDOM GOT BURNS ASHES TO ASHES AS TROYS
MEN DIED WHAT IS THE MUSE OF FIRE TRUSTIEST
ARMOR LUST OF GOLD RED ORANGE OH SOUND JULY
JET SAMPLED THATS A CRAP WAY TO FLARE OUT
FARTING UNDEFECATED MONTHS WITH NO IDEAS

XI. TOLL, KENT

My chances of being knighted grow dire. I'm fine
if I never play the Dane. My remaining years will not
be spent reading Donne by the fire in a book-lined
cottage in Kent. So I'll blow my Anglophone
about the one close to home, next exit on I-80,
where a black friend of mine, a professor, still asks
for a bag when he leaves any bookshop—so the cop
won't glance. He'll take it, he says, over Kent
in the '70s, shame of a nation, the shootings news *not*
because of the killing—killing flew—news because of
who'd killed who. All the signs at the tollbooth flash:
white on black, black on yellow, red on white.
My imaginary radio croons *Four dead in O-hi-o . . .*
but news like that, Neil Young, is old. The toll is low.

XII. LOAN, GLASGOW

Where I first learned to say things, Ohio, my accent
was the local legal tender: good in Edinburg
as Dublin or London. Then came Glasgow (proper).
One year abroad in broad Glaswegian, the notes
brought from home bouncing everywhere, overdrawn.
Want a wild time? In Glasgow time was *tame.*
See the town? You had to hear the *tune.* New loans,
including my name; I began saying *Cave-in*
if I wanted the right introduction in a pub. The road
was *rude,* the power sometimes *poor.* My voice
skim milk in that butterchurn of gutturals, Scots vowels
clotted and spread like cream, I learned to hear
everything twice and nothing the same. Glasgow
never leaves you alone: it leaves you *a lane.*

XIII. FLIGHT, ATHENS

Just a few hours from Oxford, as the crow flies,
my crow back then was any Eagle Talon out of town
bearing down hard on Halloween, Ohio-U-style,
annual tri-state bender of a weekend. And who
to be headed straight for in that mid-fall, Midwest
Mardi Gras? Terence "Uber" Huber, man of
a thousand nicknames: tales of insane asylums,
a pentagram of graveyards, the lost school of found poems
Athens is. We'd booze it up, talk smack, talk shop,
stumble back to his place sloppy and break out
the high school mag, our fledgling efforts, *Flight*,
for a laugh. Goliards big on talk, maybe small
on cash . . . those nights were Ohio to me—Terry's couch—
a place where until you could fly, you could crash.

XIV. SQUARING-THE-CIRCLE, EUCLID

Something about the square we can manage:
an area arrived at by one side, a body built
entire from a single rib. A finite, fine idea.
We dwell with it. Something about the circle's
more otherworldly, can't be hacked: to grasp it,
we had to invent a figure akin to intuition.
The classical problem arose (beyond hubris,
well past incest): could a square area be extracted,
perfectly, from a circle? Anaxagoras couldn't see it
anywhere, especially not the floor of his prison.
Thought impossible for centuries, finally *proven*
impossible the day that pi was deemed so damned
transcendental. O radius, you jab in the rib,
we still don't know just what you're up against.

XV. OMISSION, CLEVELAND

When did I notice you begin at *C level?*
All those years I drove into you, the letters must
have slipped me some sooth—though I know, I know,
you rise above it. Still, C level fits:
the even keel, average but no slacker, with so little
need for an *A* that you dropped one early on from
your composing sticks, Moses's CLE*A*VELAND
squeezed in the interest of space. And somewhere
in one of your synagogues, a Kabbalist knows
how much can hang on one letter: one omission
from the Talmud will end creation, boil the seas,
set every river on fire. You're a warning—or confession—
I never could finish. *C level and* . . . and what?
Open question.

XVI. INDIGNITY, BROKENSWORD

Indignity, to weep by your own weapons.
Lore has it that a captured cavalry colonel
plunged his sword into the clay-cool creekbank
and snapped it at the hilt, not wanting to be bled
by his own blade. Heroic stuff. The natives
burned Col. Crawford, stuff and all, at the stake,
touched their torches and glared (less well-kept,
but undoubtedly there, what set his captors off).
Namesake not of the soldier, nor his fate,
nor of those who sparked this token break.
Now each May, or Mays when anyone cares,
spring arrives with a senior prank—
another spraypaint spoiler to whom it occurs
BROKEN can stay BROKEN, SWORD become WORD.

XVII. EUCHRE, AKRON

The only shuffle quick enough for breaks,
think of the Akron factory rules: no table talk,
card-laid-card-played, dismissed from the deal
if you take all day, a new next waiting behind your chair
like a carrion bird or a communicant. Nowhere else
so loved as the Midwest, where you'd better have
in euchre—like sex—a good partner or a good hand.
Here the name of the game is dashing hope:
one point for calling and following up, but *two*
for punishing the other team's ambitions.
It's euchre to put a false prophet in his place,
trump his ace, nail that thief-redeemer to
a crucifix, no tricks. As poet dealt to poet once:
some play euchre, some play Eucharist.

XVIII. APHORISMS, SOLON

Less is more, more or less: never attach an epigraph
that's better than the poem. Might as well give
a butterfly cement antennae. Better to swallow
the bugger whole; better yet, dress it up in such
filament they'll forget how it came to your web—
and vampirize. Some call this "spin."
Some "design." The Greek Solon made laws sound
like cobwebs—good for catching trifling matters,
tearing when anything weightier went through them.
An epigraph of that might cut right through.
We just don't MAKE IT NEW like we used to, or,
as elder poets said, don't trust anyone over thirty
lines. Less-ons are for pessimists, so the optimist teaches
mor-ons. Shouldn't someone be writing this down?

XIX. EROSION, CIRCLEVILLE

A boulder. Shows. How nature. Fights the right-
angle: tenderness toward every edge; for every sharp,
a correspondent soothe. The sagged stone stair worn
of waiting. Corners take the block nowhere, it wants
to wheel any direction, go rolling. You there, you
turning curves into squares, try Rome and its hills.
Try Cincinnati. Or try Circleville, the berg you've never
heard of, try the prehistoric mounds it settled in.
A circular town looked so good on paper.
Folks came to see. With steam. But the avenues proved
difficult, for carriages, for commerce. Arc by arc,
old earthwalls removed, the circular squarely voted
down. Today no vestige left. Like anyone
can resist. An edge. Like any. Other. Town.

XX. Y-BRIDGE, ZANESVILLE

The highway alphabet game has brought you here
(from Akron, Barberton, Canton) to the famous
Y of Z, a find, and hard to find many like it in the world—
until the world gets wise. Would Pythagoras
think this divine? Would he bring disciples by
for clandestine rites while skeptical citizens slept?
One road to Getaway, Pleasantville, and Rich Valley;
one to Rocky Ridge, Plain City, and Freedom.
Choose. . . . Today people don't rule out soul-transmigration,
and yeah it's still hard telling symbols from things,
but scan the local skyline and you don't see many
Pythagorean steeples. Cite what you like: prohibitions
against eating hearts or beans, against picking up
what has fallen, against walking a well-known road.

Statue

I. JULY 9, 1776

State is what it stands for: standing.
More power, that said, to statue. Topple
base topple legs topple torso topple top,
et cetera, all that glop. All that glitz
is not gold. All that gilt
is. Have you pulled and stripped
the emperor's new clothes? Now what?
The belly of said statue, lead, makes
many thousand musket rounds. Put them
in your smoke and pipe them, your lordship,
your highness. (Gunsmoke. Bagpipe.
Filed-by-firelight tax returns.) United,
we state, united we topple topple.
Domino once stood for lord.

II. APRIL 9, 2003

It's televised. It's technically a knockout:
Saddam gets dragged around the ring. His minister
gives our newsmen a yuk, a ha, and a ho
befitting such heaves: "Everything's under control."
Please. We've seen these stands before; they stand
no chance against our democratic dance of tanks
and you're welcome. Got him over a barrel.
Tons. And while we know he's full of gas,
we're not too sure the spokesman back home is better:
war tongue-in-cheek and foot-in-door, a species
of arguing Socrates critiqued, good at knocking
any case down, then collapsing on itself.
Look again and it's George up there, under control
as ever, a TV-policeman posing for his bust.

Another Untied Shoe

Recalling the Sting Bible, an edition published in 1746, in which Mark 7:35 has "the sting of his tongue" instead of "string"

The ungulfed gap between
the poem and the idea
(somewhere is no rope
to measure it)

          between the *wind* and the *mind*

Difference slim, (a) letter thin

          between the *nomen* and the *omen*

Yet significant (one
tosses in bed and finds,
to disappointment, half
the beast asleep)

          between the *sheen* and the *sheet*
          between the *flash* and the *flesh*

Outline begs
to live beyond its means

          between the *root* and the *roof*
          between the *wood* and the *word*

How many ancient tongues
knew wood as wisdom

          between a *wreath* and a *breath*

Thick ring here shows
rain was good (that year)

          between the *dear* and the *dead*

Does holding (even)
hold?

           Between the *stranger* and the *strangler*
           between the *rope* and the *rape*

Grinning our teeth, grinding our teeth

           between the *lawful* and the *awful*

(All for naught)
and naughtiness for all

           between the *formal* and the *normal*

I do not ask
for the title (I ask
for the book)

           between the *called* and the *culled*
           between the *soil* and the *soul*

Why rend?
Why rend(er)?

           between *decision* and *derision*
           between the *pretty* and the *petty*

The (perpendicular
at tangent) pin asks
too much of its balloon

           between the *snob* and the *slob*
           between the *walk* and the *talk*

Something we see everyday
beneath (the ground) or within
(another untied shoe)

           between the *ill* and the *pill*
           between our *woes* and our *wows*

To have to stoop to
(me and my fair-weather saints)

           between the *paint* and the *pain*
           between the *mute* and the *muse*
           between our *lies* and our *lines*

(Parentheses work
like dimples around a smirk)
        between the *versified* and the *verified*
        between *seedtime* and *weedtime*
Significant
(inside it:
if I can
and
if I can't)
Worth noting
Worth nothing
        between the *herd* and the *head*
Great finds, great minds
and subtle serendipity
        between the *warming* and the *warning*
Captain (who kept his beer
near the cool keel of his ship)
discovered the Gulf Stream
(when all went bad)
        between the *bitter* and the *better*
We get no holiday for this
        between a *fast* and a *feast*
(The world wants what?) A new
neurosis every now and then
        between the *sickness* and the *slickness*
        between the *oil* and the *soil*
Burning (like) an unloosed truth
        between the *om* and the *um*
Off-guard in the garden
        between the *ample* and the *apple*
The power of (holding)
a moment in a name
        between the *worm* and the *word*

The blame
(or maybe reward)
for loss of limb, of life
of language

                between the *shape* and the *shame*

                between the *bonus* and the *onus*

What did you learn at the feet
of the rebbe? (Life
in the tying of laces)

                between the *string* and the *spring*

Twist that talks
(discover a name for God
and never speak it)

                between the *sainted* and the *tainted*

                between the *trusty* and the *rusty*

                between the *willing* and the *wilting*

Hunters and gatherers
Grunters blatherers

                between the *work* and the *word*

The lowest form of humor
(the wink's the lowest form of flirting)
til you use it

                between the *wit* and the *twit*

                between the *witless* and the *witness*

Seeing through the dim-to-dark

                between the *certain* and the *curtain*

The curtain parts
the mind is taken off (a prop,
a shirt too often worn) you

                between the *natal* and the *fatal*

                between *germination* and *termination*

Feel the *carry* in vicarious
and are born

        between the *friend* and the *fiend*

Into a (yes-where-we-left-it)
scene of envoys, enemies,
go-betweens

        between the *champ* and the *chump*

(Battle alarms
violence off)

        between the *glory* and the *gory*
        between the *danger* and the *anger*

Like *Prometheus* of
Euripides where no
one does (but sees)

        between the *torch* and the *touch*

Once winked at (twice
thinked at)

        between the *touch* and the *ouch*

Culture's core picked (daily
like the lotto) O the vultures

        between the *fame* and the *flame*

(The chance to die
and take the whole
world with you)
All history
but one life long

        between *meaning* and *moaning*
        between the *clod* and the *cloud*

Alexander ruled the world
and the world ruled Alexander
(and the world)

        between the *claw* and the *law*
        between the *ravage* and the *savage*

                              between the *breast* and the *beast*
                              between
                              the *beast* and the *best* between the
                              best and the *rest*

Even here (or next to)
in the one-off bin
of pseudonyms

                              between the *literal* and the *liberal*
                              between the *myth* and the *math*

I'm going to put a
bullet in your head

                              between *defined* and *defiled*

I say bullet (*BANG!*)
it's in your head

                              between the *lord* and the *word*

(The gut the gun
the gulp the gulf
the reach the breach
the powder the power
the gap the cap
the lead the head)

                              between the *wold* and the *world*
                              between the *word* and the *world*

Because of that
how vast is possibility (spaces
between the stars)

                              between the

What we hold
on the tongue a moment we
                              do not   *do now*

Own
(it leaves us
and is ours)

It's Tarmac

Heading back home to Ohio. December 2000. I live in Virginia. This is not an essay, it's a Saturn. It's a Saturday. It's Saturnalia—nearly—it's nearly Christmas. Of the routes between Charlottesville and Brunswick, I'll take the flattest, and fastest, 400-some miles of blacktop. Between here and there is a *t*. It astounds no one—nearly. It might astound me.

———————

Barracks Road. Gassed up, grabbed a few things. Dr. Pepper and O'Henry my company. No writing for weeks, day job taking it all out of me. Which is why I brought this recorder. Why I bought a blank tape. Why I have a word in mind, and no way to get to it yet. Sometimes I can feel writing coming on, a premonition of an earthquake, a thousand rats abandoning the sewer before the shake. So this is my little rat trap. On this model, as on many, you can't engage RECORD without PLAY.

———————

Lewis-and-Clarking it, George-Rogers-Clarking it, 64 West. I promised no music, must go the distance on monologue. Indian Territory. New France. The Northwest, the Old Northwest, Middle West, Midwest. The frontier turns to Front Street. What I want is the word on the street. I want names and what becomes. Years I've wanted to put this all down. This recorder and this deposition. All roads lead.

———————

To home. One letter differences. My farther and other will be waiting. They met in grade school. He's the one in horn-rimmed glasses. She's the cute immigrant kid at the front of the room. Her maiden name (Bretmersky) was a clerical error on a baptismal certificate (Pretmersky). A flattery of my inner life is having pinned my very existence on that slip. I've disimagined myself had my parents never met up, for as many reasons as that switch could bear. Had her war-displaced family not been asked to stand in the A–M line but the N–Z and gone on to Hungarian enclaves other than Cleveland. Had the nuns of their school seated her in the back of the class instead of the front, out of dreamshot of one near-sighted schoolboy whose eyes I have inherited. One letter. Between pig Latin and big Latin. Between praying and braying.

John Loudon McAdam invented the modern road building process. When his father died during his adolescence, McAdam was sent to America to live with his uncle, where he accumulated a fortune. Not honestly, is the impression I get. A Tory, he lost some of his property during the American Revolution, but returned to Scotland wealthy and at some level a believer in the American new man. Many Adamses in the young republic.

"North Americans have tended to confuse human fate with their own salvation. In this I am North American."—Susan Howe. And how. In this I am in agreement, that is, confusion. I mean to mislead a little. An unseen Auditor is already reckoning my bad logic: mother's B-name would put her farther in any seating chart from McFadden than a P-name—it doesn't follow. What can I say. If you're going to think like that this won't be any fun. Auditor to my oddity.

Blacktop a misnomer this time of year. Snowplows have worked the roads white through the night. Bottoms up: how cars grow salty, like biblical or Ovidian transformations. The Romans are never too far from my mind. The streets of America paved with gold, if your salary is salt. All loads read.

A green sign reads CHRISTIANS CREEK. The state won't spring for an apostrophe. Christian possessive or Christians plural? Confusion omission makes.

---

81 North. *Y* is Pythagoras' letter—or upsilon was—a path which branches toward virtue or vice. Puns too work off convergence. Beware of punsters: born conciliators, more alive to what brings together than what drives apart.

Staunton, Virginia: birthplace of Woodrow Wilson. Virginia is the mother of presidents, eight, more than any other state. I grew up in Ohio, mother of presidents, eight, more than any other state. Tourist bureaus could confer. Claims, clams. Virginia is for lovers. Ohio is for loners.

The centuries agree with each other in one regard: turning men into dust. Save the nineteenth. The industrial century delighted in reducing men to verbs. To lynch. To boycott. To galvanize. Plenty more turned to nouns. The newton. The watt. The volt. Who needs the divine, Ovid, with more mundane metamorphoses within a century or so of reach? And the surface over which we glide, macadam.

Ox, house, camel—oldest ABCs—read like any manger scene along the highway. Some comfort in the letters. Taken from the world, I like to think there is some low voltage from the dawn of civilization still running through their simple and infinitely interchangeable lines, loops and diagonals. I like to think. Proto-semitic ideogrammatic meanings (door, man praying, nail) submerged during the Babylonian exile. Phoenician, Greek, Roman, the Auditor knows the story, I needn't repeat it. Now mostly learned for sounds. The O in "O'Henry" stares me down.

Romans prized accomplished orators, lawyers, rhetoricians, those able to defend either side of the road. To take here and make it there. To take there and make it here. Accomplishment in Roman cuisine (this is neither here nor there) was to take fish and make it look like fowl. Fowl like beast. When Ovid gets cooking, he can serve anything up plausibly. Don't guard your wife, she must guard herself to be true; guard your wife to make the adultery tempting. Ovid didn't use the iamb, but the ambi: his ambidexterity, his ambivalence. And what does it take to make a falsity look suddenly true? Ambition.

———

My brothers will be home when I arrive. Two Ph.D.s—one a Classicist, one a Medievalist. Mealtime conversation at the McFaddens' was once described as watching Anglo-Saxon and Romance languages wrestle for the rights to English. In Latin road (*via*) and life (*vita*) are separated by one letter—like *nomen omen*. Road comes from the Old English *rode,* variously meaning tree trunk, branch, club, measuring stick, safe shelter, or crucifix. Christ calls himself the way, the truth, and the life—*via, veritas, vita*—excellent rhetorical progression for a language he did not speak. Reminiscent of *Veni, vidi, vici*—one J.C. to another. Et tu, Jude? Surly comes from sir. Hard to read the Bible linearly, given the two different accounts of Genesis and Judas's death. Punctuation is piercing. My mom and dad, blowing on their ham bone soup, exchange glances of middle-class pride over the three amusing linguistocrats they've created. Do another, I can hear my father ask. Do the one about the horse.

———

Omission confusion makes: a sign says BLACKS RUN. Still in the South, the Auditor reminds, waiting for the joke. We don't have humor, or not much humor, without fear. Taboo, bad taste, the wrong song, something deserving of an exile, the spike in the punch. I pass over Blacks Run. When I grew up, grammarians had us diagram sentences. I'd have learned more between now and then had I learned to diagram jokes. In the predicate punchline, there's always (below the line which gets said) the dotted line which can't get said, or no joke. I think about that line a little, its gap, its gasp, whenever I'm amused. Indelicate object.

———

The "one about the horse" is an obscure little monograph in two voices, my brothers' voices, regarded as the most famous of the McFadden dinner dialogues. Its purpose was to demonstrate how common words tend to replace the more formal as a language evolves. Pat puts forth the lowerclass *caballus* and the standard *equus*. *Equus* is the only word found in Roman high genres, yet it is effectively extinct in the modern Romance languages. *Caballus,* on the other hand, has survived it in the Italian *cavallo,* French *cheval,* and the Spanish *caballo.* Brian interjects that *horse* comes from a Germanic root, everyday diction, whereas "cavalry" and "equestrian" lived on in more formal terms, legal and ecclesiastical documents—so, again, an upperclass / lowerclass distinction. My part in the dialogue is the silent one, like the photographer's part in a portrait.

———

Vanity is a lot less expensive in Virginia. So far today I've seen HERTOY, PAID 4, and YS GUY. Personality measured in cars, engines measured in horses, horses measured in hands. If I could retroactively penetrate the one about the horse, I would interject a false etymology. *Kabbala* from *caballus.* Or *caballus* from *Kabbala,* a convincing case for either way.

———

Horseplay behooves me.

———

Past Harrisonburg; by now I know the rest of the trip will be as vainglorious, I've driven it enough. Toms Brook. Stephens City. Geography, like history, written from Victorsville. The Vandals made a name for themselves too, but their version wasn't vandalism. How names stick.

———

How names *tick.* Etymology and pun have been called twins, though only one is deemed legitimate. Etymology gets grins, the pun groans. Why? Puns understandable, but not rational. They do what Newton said couldn't be done: two bodies, same space, same time. Two or more. Intuitive etymologies: that's what good puns intend to be. Sound arguments. The Irish, restyled lately as the saviors of Western civilization, were devotees of etymology in the Middle Ages, when the science of philology was murky at best. From intuitive etymologists like Isidore of Seville, the Irish kept the tradition that *equus* comes from equal.

Three crosses by the side of the road. Calvary, cavalry. Freud retells the joke of two underhanded American businessmen seeking to gain access to high society by having expensive portraits of themselves painted. An art critic points to the empty space on the wall between the two likenesses, asking, "And where is the Savior?"

Surface a little slick. There's nothing quite like the sensation of recovering from a skid: you steer into the fear. I press on into winter. When the Church chose the solstice as the date for Christmas, it was layering Christ over Saturn, a Roman layering over the Greek Chronos, a combination of Cronus (the Reaper) and Kronos (Time). Apparently, the Greek names sounded so alike that the two became one frequent association. In the painting under the painting, Father Time got his scythe from a slip of the tongue.

Pavement under the pavement. See *Roman Roads,* by Chevallier. McAdam knew some Roman roads, a few of which were and are still traceable in Britain; Rome's road knowledge, however, had crumbled with the empire, placing the burden of repair and construction on whichever feudal powers could or would see to them. Road making in the Britain of McAdam's youth was not much more advanced, abandoned to individual counties and parishes. In grad school back in Charlottesville, I once found a microfiche of McAdam's *Practical Essay on the Scientific Repair and Preservation of Roads.* I made copies and kept it in a drawer. I would pull it out once in a while to see what his words might mean to me, or just to listen to him whine about the shabbiness of road conditions. "It is generally deemed sufficient," he lamented, "to collect a considerable quantity of stone or gravel, and to throw it down upon the ground."

Romans great travelers too. Seneca the name of an Indian tribe and a Roman philosopher. "You are surprised that you have made such a long journey and by such a variety of routes, yet you have not dispelled the gloomy weariness within your heart? You need a change of soul, not of clime." Which speaks? No matter, Seneca. We're still with ourselves.

I pass Edinburg . . . no *h*, no burr, soft ending hardened in transit. Little known fact: McAdam was a descendant of the clan MacGregor, and when the clan name was outlawed, a certain Adam from his line settled in the lowlands and changed his name to McAdam. The knack for complete reinvention. Adam McAdam, the self-made man, slate wiped clean. To start from scratch, from A.

"Artless, unstoried, unenhanced." How off was Frost. In the last ten years, evidence has been building to retrace in Ohio the Great Hopewell Road, the planned holy road of a lost civilization. A long path 200 feet wide and banked on either side by mounds. These mounds and many like it fill the Mississippi watershed as evidence of a lost way of life. La Salle, the first European to completely explore this region, came after ten years in the Jesuit order. Jesuits were known to be great talkers, another word for everything. *America* and *wilderness* were synonyms. La Salle's other name was Cavelier. In a time when exploration was synonymous with colonization, he could claim the entire Mississippi basin with just one: *France.*

Any trace of self-conscious wordplay in antiquity, the traditional argument runs, is probably coincidental; the ancients are straightforward, sincere, sober. Any assertion that words were central, that wordplay might have been a structural element of style and content, is denounced as retroactive deviance from original authorial intention. Sober bores. Who's more sober than Virgil? In Chapter VIII of *The Aeneid,* Virgil writes Saturn "preferred the place be called Latium because he had hidden safe on these shores." When you consider Latium is both an anagram of *maluit* ("he preferred") and a permutation of *latuisset* ("he had hidden") . . . coincidence doesn't seem to cover it. And think of Biblical wordplay, Adam sounding like the Hebrew word for *man,* Eve sounding like *living,* Cain sounding like *gotten.* Read through Genesis with substitutions and it's more allegorically rich: Man named his companion Living, the Lord rejects the offering of Gotten.

As a trustee of Scottish roads, McAdam investigated highways all over Britain and arrived at the conclusion that the best roads were made of broken stone that could be compacted into place, larger stones laying a foundation for smaller. Highest point in the middle for drainage. He began putting his theories into practice as surveyor general of Bristol, and published his *Practical Essay.* By this time, "macadamisation" was sweeping Britain. He was soon appointed by Parliament the General Surveyor of Roads. Offered a knighthood, he declined.

Jesuitical means "equivocal," a probably-not-undeserved epithet leveled at the Jesuit order by its enemies because some of their early moralists taught that the end ("the Greater Glory of God") justifies the means. Great confusers of their congregations, sophistic, hairsplitting. So bad a pope even banned them. If you count the marks of the Church as One, Holy, Catholic, and Apostolic, the kind of Jesuit in question couldn't count past One.

There aren't really spaces between words, not in the air anyway, not when it's up and running. Who can tell "Jesus wept" from "Jesus swept?"

Satire not from *satyr,* as the English Renaissance believed. A *satura* is a mixed dish. Related sides: satisfied, saturated, Saturn—god of plenty, the golden age. Latium is the region around and including Rome, the earthly exile where the dethroned Saturn hid from Jove. We get Latin from hiding.

———

At midnight on Christmas, legend holds, the oxen are given the gift of speech. Hardy would believe again if they would only kneel. I'll transcribe this dictation during the holidays. I'll strip. Embellish. Fill out any quotes I've butchered. I'll sit at my laptop and hope for the zone of synthesis with the machine: infiltration, immersion, entering its grid of chips so fully and efficiently that I lose time, feel as if I write and think directly into its memory. Do we become one with our devices, as mounted Mongols and Spaniards were thought to be one with their horses? Union with an inanimate object is a deception, like the illusion of yourself somewhere behind a mirror, or, more sympathetically, in it. And still, I will type, and still, I will drive, awaiting that zone.

———

Automatic transmission. Hard drive.

———

Is it sufficient to leave these heaps? Of course abstractions are real, they're real abstractions. I'm interested in how thoughts cluster around a word. Its real bones and its ghost limbs. Any word. Death. State. Statistic. Etymology, emphasis, pronunciation of words. "A language is a dialect with an army and a navy."—Max Weinreich. A dialect is a citadel. Approaching the word as a mandala, square within circle within square, Adam within Adam within within within within. We often take circumlocution as evasion, it needn't be. It might be a first step, a first form, trianguluation: talk around something long enough and you can divine its center. Circumlocation. Perigraphs. I am going somewhere. Essay is related to exact, but this is not an essay. You Essay. My word.

———

When someone is thinking we say, "The wheels are turning."

"Poets that Lasting Marble seek / Must carve in Latin or in Greek; / We write in Sand." Just a poet again, contemning the contemporary. And still we quote Waller. And still we go on, speaking a language, writing poems on a surface that's shifting under our feet. PC personal computer or PC politically correct? Sand's fine at least. We grovel in gravel.

There were plenty of words for horse in Old English poetry probably due to the needs of alliteration. I've heard that in English the word with the most synonyms or idioms is *drunk*. Probably due to the needs of poets.

A formalist is a moral fist.

Jokes explained cease to be jokes. Become what then, criticism? Joke the Medievalist once told me by way of Charles the Bald: "What's the difference between a *Scotus* and a *sotus* (an Irishman and a drunk)?" The answer isn't C. The punchline is *Tanta tabula* or "Only a table." It has something to do with being drunk under one, proclivities of the Scottish-Irish line. And there the joke goes down the steep and musty cellar-stair to criticism.

Winchester trying hard to hide the Roman *castra* in its name. I spy. The streets of America paved in grids: easily managed, defended, extended. Rome (the city) began organically, but Rome (the idea) set the T-square on Gaul, Britain, and North Africa. With the grid, control of conquered territory was possible, and the colonization of war veterans. Colony comes from farmer. Another name for the part of Ohio I'm going to be going through: the Western Reserve.

"Going to"—an odd future form. "Going to stay" is paradoxical. Like "had lost."

Creation invites reaction. Why does God reject the offering of Cain? Mysterious ways. No reason is explicit in Genesis, though we theorize. God prefers sheep to corn, nomads to farmers. Inconclusive. God chooses Abel, Cain chooses murder, and for killing a nomad, Cain is made one. Why won't God take both offerings? A basic tenet of monotheism holds there can be only one blessing and it is better not to beg such questions. Ask Esau. Saturn the sower too was deposed.

Author comes from "grower." Quintillian warns against double-entendre in *Instructing the Orator,* its potential to undermine the author. Johnson, Voltaire, Dryden, Pope all pronounced themselves enemies of the pun (and used them). Puns aren't natural; they are mannered, self-conscious, innately "verbal" and therefore not "real." I'm not sure when the word first began its exile from the realm of the natural world, but I suspect it was around the time humans began deciding we weren't a part of it either. Any beast knows how to give the signal "Run"; but when we had mastered "Run home, get two spears and meet me at the river," we might have seen our lot and the beasts' diverge. As if by magic. Word as power. You can imagine that defenders of the language (the Augustans saw the first English dictionaries) would be troubled by any obstacle to the ideal language with no miscommunication. A pun represents the irresolvable command, botched plot, paradox which makes the mandatory damnatory. Bane of the hunting-and-gathering set, the right-of-way crowd, divine-right, right-of-kings. Eminent domain. I'm passing out of the Old Dominion. On a run and a pun.

West Virginia. Four signs on the right side of the road, 200 feet apart: "Skies of blue / Fields of green / Our mountain state / Keep it clean!" Litterature. Is a joke a joke if no one is there to hear it? Freud is clear on the point: yes and no.

"The noblest prospect which a Scotchman ever sees is the road that leads him to England!"—Samuel Johnson. Johnson's dictionary included a definition for oats: a grain given "to horses in England and people in Scotland." At the end of the *Practical Essay,* McAdam claims that after working for a while in the difficulties of his profession, he no longer considers himself up to the task, but lobbies for the employment of "officers of education in character" to continue the labors of road reform. Scottish in the world of English gentlemen, he complains of the "obstacles of prejudice and ignorance, which nothing but time and talent, exerted under the fostering care of the Legislature, can effectually overcome." Read him sometime. You'll spot his predilection for Latinates, the power words. McAdam would have been familiar with Johnson's dictionary. *See* DUNCE.

HARPERS FERRY. I don't take this route for history, but history slips in, with my father's voice and his sad eyes. During Roman Saturnalia, according to a satire of Horace, there was a custom by which a slave may address his master with impunity. Was it strange for Horace to own a slave, his father, after all, a freedman? What do you call that voice in your head that tells you you are a pretender in Caesar's court? I wonder what McAdam called it. I'll keep calling it the Auditor.

I don't know what rhyme, alliteration, and assonance are except descriptions of puns. Agents of the irrational. Used to be "Neither rhyme nor reason"—implying opposition. Now rhyme is described as the "law of return." Alliteration and assonance are structured coincidences between words. I'm not sure how rhyme, alliteration, and assonance became white and pun remained colored, but the distinction, after any degree of inspection, is ridiculous. Rhyme is a pun with a Mary and a navy. My Saturn hums.

NATURALIZED AREA, whatever that means. My mother was naturalized. No Hungarian for me, only a few household words and admonitions. Other children were naughty, I was *csúnya*. Other children had snot, I had *cigány*. Years before we discovered that cigány was a slur, literally "gypsy." I once told my mother I wasn't coming home because—I got this from Ovid—home was "a narrow stall." I was presumably the stallion too long in it. Made her cry that day. Glasgow, San Francisco, Virginia . . . I'm still that little snot.

In the hall of punsters reclines Heraclitus, retelling his best: *The bow means life but its target is death.* In Greek, bow (*bios*) and life (bi*os*) are spelled the same, differing emphasis. I've found "pass on" is a difficult phrase. I'll *pass* on that. I'll *pass on* that.

Potomac River. Downstream, a city planned in the grand style. L'Enfant's baby, child of a child. L'Enfant wanted more than the grid. He wanted to Versailles the eye: axials, fountains, the Tiber Creek diverted to flow in waterfalls along the Capitol steps. The Tiber a too-obvious rhyme. His Washington was a city never fully realized, but it at least beat Jefferson's proposal, a timidly gridded structure without any of the sweep and magnificence. Jefferson in turn unleashed his squares westward: the Northwest Ordinance was based on his model. *Barracks* and *barrio* are related. Grids appear in ancient cities of imperial China and Japan. Babylon, says Herodotus, had rectilinear streets and canals.

I pass Antietam thinking about agreement. "Is our children learning?" President Bush has poor agreement: "Drug therapies are replacing a lot of medicines as we used to know it." He thinks while talking, and occasionally one activity distracts the other. The results are unfinished, unfinishable. Oftentimes, he changes directions midsentence and finds himself stringing together clauses no syntax can sensibly contain. A self-styled "uniter," he doesn't come to it comfortably. "Families is where our nation finds hope." Bushisms is the State of the Union.

———————

At the turnoff ramp for 70 West, a truck accident: eighteen wheels flipped completely over, a long trailer flank ripped open. A minute down the road, I see a deer by the side of the road, bleeding its freight.

———————

Pi is a pun. Transcendent and estimable, pi is a riddle we live with. To grid and to gird both imply control, one by charting and the other by surrounding. That which may be contained may be defined. Rectitude is certitude. Girth makes right.

———————

"The very idea that all is pun, a play of syllables," says Montale, "is the most credible." Spaces between words are hard to pick up when you're learning a foreign language. When I first heard French I couldn't tell where one ended and another began. *Je t'adore* was "shut a door" for all I heard. My brothers found it funny that the Scots taught me French. "Ah Bee Cee Dee . . . you know . . . like dee of the week." When Glasgow was named culture city of Europe in 1990, the only city more surprised than Edinburgh was Glasgow. I remember the city slogan was "Glasgow's Miles Better." *Better than what?* was the supposed question and *Better than Edinburgh* the supposed answer.

———————

A shortcut to the Pennsylvania Turnpike, Route 40 traces the first federally funded National Road. And the Auditor thought we'd left Jefferson at home. Jefferson pushed this road from the East to the Ohio River, and beyond, following a military path used by Braddock and Washington. Jefferson believed that the Indians could be convinced to give up their hunting and horticulture for proprietary agriculture. "But should any tribe refuse the proffered hand and take up the hatchet," he said to his Indian Territory governor, "it will be driven across the Mississippi and the whole of its lands confiscated." The etymology of *Yankee* is disputed. *Yank,* we know, means to pull away forcibly.

———————

At the Mason Dixon line, I'm still on agreement. United States are, United States is. Grammar drifts. Longinus says the contraction of plurals to singulars has the great effect of sublimity, imposing solidity, unexpected surprise. Do public words define and determine future actions of a people, or confirm their reigning assumptions? Longinus also holds that turning singulars into plurals plays into exaggeration. We need more Longinuses.

———————

As a carriage wheel passed over one end of a large stone, it kicked the other end up, making trouble for both road and carriage. McAdam was sure that large stones were responsible for the bad state of roads in Britain and insisted that stones be small enough to fit in a workman's mouth. It was once reported that he visited a site to inspect the work of one of his gangs, and found a stretch with stones too large for his specifications. When the workman was admonished, he grinned and revealed his toothless smile.

———————

"Glasgow's Miles Better," I remember, could be shown to read, "Glasgow sMiles Better."

———————

What's the difference between an Irishman and a Scot? This time the answer is *sea.* One that long has carried the mix and match of *Mc*s to *Mac*s. On the Isle of Ioná, the self-exiled St. Columba took a Gaelic name that meant "Back to Ireland"—that is, his back *turned* to Ireland. In English, the pun is diverting; "Back to" could also mean "returning to." I think of that hermit tradition often, stone huts, elected exile.

———————

Back to the tradition.

———————

A prevalent folk etymology of the word "posh" says it came from the acronym POSH stamped on tickets booked on the landward, shady cabins of steamers bound between England and India: Port Out Starboard Home. No evidence to support the claim, yet it sticks irresistibly to our sense of class. Since this is folly anyway, I imagine those on the other side of the ship, the ones resourceful or clever enough to accompany the elites but whose station kept them across the hall, the Indian manservants, black mammies, Greek teachers of Roman brats, the Starboard Out Port Homers. *Soph* stands for wisdom. Doesn't fall for Sophists.

The mountains place their winter want ad for a pastoralist. I don't apply; it's words from here to home. I don't know much Italian, another family language paved over. I do know Dante once punned the Italian for man, *omo,* with the appearance of a human face: eye, nostrils, eye. In the *Divine Comedy,* he greets a friend whose *m,* he says, he would recognize anywhere. I tilt my head back and try to read the man in the rearview mirror. Pray for the Fool's Paradise.

Breezewood is a caricature of a crossroads, entrance to the Pennsylvania pike. *Turnpike* used to mean just the roadblock, the turnstile; now the whole road. Like when people called language *grammar*—a part for a much greater whole. Grammar's the most efficient from here to there. No one lives on a turnpike, though.

Three-way intersections were supposed to be significant of ill-fate and witchcraft. Oedipus killed his father in a three-way. So to speak. Like the Trevi. The Romans introduced the habit of keeping to the left in traffic, so that carriages would pass sword arm to sword arm. This custom usually forced peasant pedestrians to the right, and was continued until the French Revolution, when which side of the road you were on became, literally, a class consideration. Robespierre raged and the carriages moved. The first "keep right" law was applied to the Pennsylvania Turnpike, after the American visits of La Fayette.

"All strategic roads were built by tyrants—for the Romans, the Prussians, or the French. They go straight across the country. All other roads wind like processions and waste everybody's time."

—Adolf Hitler. He also said he learned a lot about terror from the Jesuits. Black uniforms, specious reasoning, unquestioning obedience, terrorism of the conscience.

Ever hear of the Walking Treaty incident? It is an interpretation of a treaty between William Penn and the Delawares entitling Pennsylvania to lands west and north of the Delaware river, in the treaty's words, "as far as a man can go in a day and a half"—probably meant to be around 30 miles. The people of Pennsylvania, with available land filling up, set to making a straight path nearly due west from the furthest inland bend of the river. Then they chose a runner of excellent stamina and set him running one minute after midnight. At 36 hours, he collapsed 150 miles inland. The native villages in this region were then abandoned, reluctantly, in keeping with the bargain they had made. Literal thinking, lateral thinking. Yankee ingenuity.

Language is a tar pit. All our ancient monsters stuck in it. All our secrets. In Latin, the idiom was not "make a plan," but "take a plan"—as if a plan exists already, an abstraction from above which may be plucked at any time from the ether. The Roman reputation as the thug-thieves of civilization makes all their accomplishments booty. You have to give them the arch, though: a curve with the strength of a square. If they took that, it had to come from beyond.

How can one read the Ecclesiast's "So remember your Creator while you are still young" without knowing that *your Creator* sounds like the ancient Hebrew for *your grave*? How is this something we've stopped taking into account? If I die in a car crash, this recording would serve as a black box, last words. This recording has the premeditation and calculation of a suicide note, it occurs to me. Just in case, folks, it is not.

46

Can't turn *saturn* to *nature* because I can't turn *s* to *e*. Still so much ground to cover. Our words as our roads, narrowing, widening. The word *deer* was once Old English for any four-legged beast; now it is specific. Ford was once a very particular man and now he has morphed into any of his automobiles. Ford has widened and deer narrowed. Ford is wolf to deer, go figure.

Mac was a nickname I grew up on. An everyman, a buddy, a joe. A favorite of football coaches at my Catholic high school: "Nice block, Mac," "Come on, Mac, some effort." Ethnicity, identity; the roster seemed to hold the same heraldries each year. Son of Fadden. Son of Gregor. For the first few weeks of training camp each summer, we wore those names on our helmets, black marker on athletic tape, so the coaches would know who they were shouting at. O'Boyle. Dawson. Patronymics that coaches could play on in their prodding. "Too many pierogies this summer, Wisneski?" "You're slow, Di Gregorio, lay off the pasta." When we were conditioned enough to start hitting, those fixes were the first victims. One good collision could strip the *Mc* right off. Or break your *ski*. Or clip your *son*.

Johnstown exit. Flood, of old. Monism has its moments. This isn't one of them. When you're preparing for the catastrophe, think like God, like Noah. Two of everything.

"Which way was vice introduced . . . if not the road?"—Pliny the Elder. The old alibi, the fatherland is pure, evils come through customs. Groups maintain their identity by delimiting the books the group is supposed to read, even the words used. Canonists, sanctions. It interests me that the selected books which comprise the Hebrew Scriptures have been revisited—by Jews and Christians alike—in periods when a threat to group identity has been made. The first Roman satirist made a spelling primer to guard against—*ironia ironiarum*—intrusive Greekisms.

I'm still catholic. Small c. Capitalization makes a difference—consider a big-C Coke habit versus a small-c coke habit—it makes a difference. *Bible,* no matter what C you choose, means "books" not "book." One story unfolding? The quest for one leads people to elaborate prefigurements and strained typologies: Abel is a Christ, killed by his brothers; Joseph is a Christ, sold for silver; Samson is a Christ, self-sacrificed. Foreshadowing, God, we get it. One tree atones for another. But my kind doesn't find salvation in a story. I find it where the word halts, breaks in two, two or more, and immensity sets in. Wolf in the flow. Jesus made puns not just parables. World without beginning middle end: Amen.

What's your hurry? he says doing 70. The automotive leap is from zero to 60; for Pascal it was zero to one. Speed-reading, yes, but you don't see slow-reading courses much. The Classicist reads slowly, and he's the one who knows six languages. That we learn to *read past* individual words to get to an overarching meaning is an unfortunate setback. A lot to learn when you take a word slow. We're velocitized.

Tar was later added to the macadam mixture when the high speeds of car wheels made even the compacted gravel come loose. The verb *tar* comes from Old English, "to provoke" or "incite." To *tar on.* It had this meaning long before the noun tar was used in a humiliation rite. A tar for a tar. Our founding feathers. *Tar* comes from tree.

Book comes from beech.

Ebony and phonics equals Ebonics. Phonics and ebony equals phony. Language politics is a tar pit too. Some wag concocted a gender-friendly pronoun for "he or she or it": *h'or'sh'it.* If the "one about the horse" is true, it doesn't bode well for believers in the Church of English. The peasants are storming the citadel. Can't take the stalwart grammarian too seriously when I consider that zeal is usually connected to the fear of losing the benefits of the literate classes. Between defending and depending.

———————

End of Chesapeake watershed. The Mississippi and its tributaries were the main water-road for the mound builders, from the Gulf of Mexico up to the Great Lakes. So what do we make of the landscaped Great Hopewell Road? The geometrical and astronomical alignments of the mounds show their builders were quite in tune with the natural world. Its builders were mysterious even to the American inhabitants when the white man came to this continent. This lapse in continuity is frightening. When lapses occur, explanations are first to rush in. I'm learning not to crowd lapses. To let lapses speak for themselves. Not just what they say, but what what they say says. Diagram that.

———————

Tunnel. ALLEGHENY MOUNTAIN on the face. If you feel like a part of a bloodstream when you're on a highway system, nothing like a tunnel to remind you. It's been suggested that the white man's domestication of livestock both exposed and immunized him to diseases that ravaged the natives. Him. As if just one. The Auditor interjects that the same "him" cannot be killed *and* spared. You know what I mean: the diseases killed one man but perhaps not his brother. Immunity is a blessing. One.

———————

The anagrammarian knows flirtation is filtration. Knows danger was spelled into the garden. The runt will have his turn, the nomad his monad. From this knowledge, it becomes possible to play whichever part / trap will flatter the empire. Virgil's dying wish was that *The Aeneid* be burned. Verse may serve. Verse may sever.

———————

McAdam (where did we leave McAdam?) enjoyed many spoils of his class, including the veneration of science and a contempt for the poor. In his *Practical Essay,* he laments that knowledge of science is no longer thought necessary to the profession of road making, and that it is left to the "most ignorant day laborer," "the lowest and most illiterate class of the community." I can remember a Christmas when my father was out of work my family needed a charity box of food from our church. I don't know how we got it. Did mom call a food bank or did someone call for us? I'll never ask, probably. The Auditor says he's heard my plebian pose before and finds it stock. The Auditor and I remember many more Christmases with two cars in the driveway, a feast on the table, and gifts under a tree. But ask me to think of a Christmas past, I remember that one.

———

Vote, veto: the great wordplay of democracy. This fall it was Bush and Gore on every screen. *Just like the movies,* my girlfriend noted. When it broke that a Bush commercial flashed *rat* on the screen as part of the scrolling word *democrat,* she told me it's the kind of thing that I might try in one of my poems. Rat in the rational. Rat in the irrational too, the psyche exceedingly democratic in its subliminal campaigns. I told her I'd think about it. I'm thinking about her Tennessee accent now, where wheels are wills. I'm thinking about Tecumseh's curse: violence or death to one elected in a zero year, true since 1840. It's zero outside. Double zero. If God is the Great Anagrammarian of the *Sefer Yetsirah,* what does all this spell us into?

———

Stopped into the American embassy to take a leak and get some food. I forget which brother joked, "You don't *take* a piss, you *leave* one"— the lessons of my fast-food youth. It's plastic, but we call it silverware. Mc-ify anything today, you denigrate its sense, commodify; 500 years after *maculate* began meaning "defile." I ordered a McLean for Plath, Lowell, and Sexton: all three were committed to a Boston asylum by that name. O little town of Bedlam. Immaculate conception. The McNuggets are for me. Filled the tank.

———

Word words. You've used them. Fast food or food food? A Chevy Nova or a nova nova? Word words. We repeat ourselves. For authenticity.

———

When I talk about satire, I don't mean Swift's definition—"a sort of glass, wherein beholders do generally discover everybody's face but their own"—I mean the mixed dish, the words I found in my mouth, verb mush, phoneme hash. I mean the capacity of lapse for self-betrayal. Sweetbread. Ox-tongue soup. *My* head on the plate.

The Roman word for pun is *agnominatio,* another name. Simon became Peter. Saul became Paul. There is a Catholic tradition of taking another name at confirmation, your second name, spoken before God in the hope he'll return the favor. My name is Kevin Joseph. Joseph means "he adds."

Allegheny River, Pittsburgh a barge-ride away. Cheap trick to quote Hitler, as I did before. Rhetorically speaking. Straw man or red herring? Red straw man. The Auditor has caught me steering assumptions: Hitler's name a dark power I have no business conjuring with. Especially not here. Fort Pitt. The letters between Colonel Bouquet and General Amherst passed through these woods as effortlessly as I have. The dark cursive correspondence, the little plan hatched in the summer of 1763 to "Innoculate" the enemy. Bouquet's poetic paranoia: "every Tree is become an Indian for the terrified Inhabitants." The oddest part of those letters is that the plans are discussed and decided in the postscripts. Lord Jeffrey Amherst. As I say the name, the stripped trees seem to part before me.

P.S. One of the postscripts—the smallpox order itself—is two pages long.

Saxonburg Boulevard passes over me. I have heard English called a warrior's language. It is not, not anymore at least. It's an insider's. A second-century heretical sect called the Cainites believed that all God's scourges were punished because they came from a higher, saving knowledge. They revered Eve, the Sodomites, believed in a Gospel of Judas. Perhaps Cain was not favored because of something in his blood. Something in his blood not beastly enough. Too cultivated. Framers, farmers. Unsettling, that's what it was. The way in grade school we called them "settlers."

The Classicist's dissertation was on Latin word order. Inversions in English stiff and Miltonic seem. Wordsworth warns not to use them, and uses them. "The prison into which we doom ourselves no prison is"? Frost also made claims to speaking in the vernacular, then spoke in the figurative. "The figure a poem makes"? Which? The figure makes the poem or the poem makes a figure? Frost is his forks.

Juvenal laments that when poets are silenced by authority they resort to rehashing myths. Extend that cowardice to the revival of hollow forms or the refuge of meaningish construction noise. McPoems, PC memos—what're we afraid to say?

If you want in, you must recognize clipping. Limo for limousine, bike for bicycle. Clipping's closest geological analog is erosion, attacking a cube or block of rock at its edges and corners until worn into a spheroid or an ovoid. There are cases of foreclipping on the road (caravan to van, omnibus to bus) but most commonly this erosion attacks a word at its rear. Carriage to car. Dashboard to dash.

Contemporary American poetry is fond of dichotomies. I'm feeling a little punchy, so I'll hazard my own one-two: those interested in *who* and those interested in *how*. Cults of who and schools of how. I like work that reconciles these approaches, craft and identity vital functions of each other. Irrelevant detail: my father taught me how to drive a car in the suburbs. Relevant: I learned the white Dodge. Irrelevant: I was born in the month of March. Relevant: born in the month of Charm.

Three was once thought of as the first number, one being unity, two division. Three was the integral composed of unity and division, a starting point. An interesting study of this belief is how in many languages *first* and *second* differ from their verbal counterparts *one* and *two*. Only at three do such words resemble their numeral, third, fourth, etc. Something happens around three. Triangle the first shape.

Beaver River. Adam was given the job of naming the beasts. Nouns are our business. Rats are chosen for clinical experiments because they don't vomit. Tar for roads because everything sticks to it. Rat. Tar. Art.

JORDAN RUN. In 1775, the Indians were assured that the Ohio would remain a boundary. "In perpetuity," as the phrase went—and we know how that phrase went. God gave the Hebrews land where they never toiled, towns they never built, vineyards they never planted. Most nations I know have expulsion myths to temper their conquests. Mine's about a mean, old king who lived in a big castle and demanded horrible taxes from a persecuted people. Mine's about humble origins. Perhaps you've heard it. Peasant stock.

Once. Twice. Thrice. Force.

New Stanton is the end of the Pennsylvania turnpike. Tollbooth. When ants build arches, the form emerges new each time. They didn't take it from anyone. Just happens. Ants dump bits of earth releasing pheromones which let succeeding ants know where to dump theirs. These pheromone-driven piles turn into towers. Two towers begin to lean toward each other because the pheromone scent from each draws ants to leave their soil on the side of a tower facing a rival tower. At some point, the rival towers grow so close to each other that one collapses into the other, and an arch is formed. Babel might have worked if there were two. Or three.

The fields are bleaker on this side. The discernible, foreboding white-
ness not my device. And still Ohio eases me. The Hitopadesa notes
"A foolish devotion to one's native place" as one of the obstacles to
greatness. One of six. "Women" and "dissatisfaction" too grace the
list, making just mentioning this suspicious wisdom. Every credo has
a coder. Cleric of the circle, I give what I have: an intense love for lan-
guage and intense distrust of it.

———————

Glacier Hills Service Plaza. Take this from college geology: ice that has
accumulated thirty meters thick begins to flow under its own weight.
Like consciousness, I think. Like ant arches. Strange weight of our
natures. Core samples have loosened air that was trapped 25,000 years
ago. During a spring thaw, my brother and I once saw the back end
of a squirrel frozen, midleap, in a snowdrift by the side of the road,
mashed in by a snowplow. Now I think that's what our fears will look
like to the future tense: pathetic, confused, frozen in drifts. Here's a
cold leap they'll spot in a minute: the uneducated are unworthy of the
keys to the meritocracy. In *Democratic Vistas,* Whitman said Ameri-
cans have never known what it is to bow before a superior. Perhaps.
But no one ever forgot how to regard an inferior.

———————

I'm getting tired. Music would help. Mind's been on too long. Mes-
merize. Bowdlerize. Luddite. The oersted is a unit of reluctance, one
gilbert per maxwell. Facts build up too. We write them down woolly
to get the mammoth off our chests.

———————

It occurs to me I am fluent in an ancient language—someday ancient.
English is synonymous with "spin"; *to put a little english on the ball* is
to lend it some zig, trickery, jazz, oomph. It should amaze me that I
can glide over these words, despised of immigrants and schoolchil-
dren, and claim some mastery. Tangle of irregulars. *Find* and *found,*
bind and *bound* . . . still one can *mind* without having *mound.* I once
remember seeing Great Serpent Mound as a child, vacationing in

Ohio. Another narrowing: *adder* in Old English used to mean any snake, now it's specific. Of course, the punster wants more than one meaning, always craving the *or* and the *and*. Or the *or* or the *and*. Subtract as you will, I am an adder.

––––––––––

Meander Lake. The odd characteristic of the Great Hopewell Road, I don't think I mentioned before, is that it is perfectly straight. It overcomes more than 50 miles of marsh, mountain, and stream as it keeps its needle-straight course from the Newark to the Chillicothe earthworks. Evidence of religious rites, if we believe experts. Evidence of a tyrant, if we believe Hitler. Or evidence that a line is only what it always was, a here-to-there, a portion of the great mandala we can plot. Plots within plots within plots.

––––––––––

Ant in the *tyrant*. *Man* in *mandala*.

––––––––––

I leave I-76 for I-80 West. Home stretch. "Had Cain been Scot, God would have changed his doom / Not forced him wander, but confined him home."—John Cleveland. What do I bring back this time? An interiority complex. A degree from the navel academy. I'm the fool who persists with his folly, hoping to be wise. Still too "too": clever, cute, antic. Arch. I drop these bits with my smell on them, hoping they'll fall together.

––––––––––

Jet-setters call this "flyover country," the great wastes between metropoles. The vast meanwhile. Here, we're positioned to see the irony. If there's an Ohioan to be found in any story, my father knows the connection. The sky is not the limit. Neither the moon. It's the same most places, really—in Scotland, there's typically a Scot behind anything useful. And *tarmac*—that's what it's reduced to—barely means road anymore, that's asphalt. If I hear *tarmac*, it is in a captain's reassuringly vacant voice, just before an airplane's skyward roar.

––––––––––

I have a point. You and I make a line. From there, we move into space. The charm of three, Ausonius was drawn to it. Three days in the tomb. Whenever *two or more of you* gathered in *my* name. Trinity. Trimurti. Tripitaka. Syllogism. The medieval trivium—logic, rhetoric, grammar—three roads to learning. Trivia. Tribe. Thesis, antithesis, synthesis. Freud's model of the psyche. Proximity to pi. Pyramids. How every numeral of a number divisible by three adds up to a number divisible by three. There is three.

———————

So keen was the assimilationist America of my mother's youth, for many years I forgot she was Hungarian at all. Cioran called Hungarian "a language in which one should expire, or renounce dying." He felt the Mongol hordes stirring in it—resembling no language in Europe. Like Nietzsche, he admired nomads, the freedom of mind which comes from changes of place. And changes of oppressors. Tartars. I've done my homework away from home. I've wondered what to do with all this. I've discovered that in Japanese Katakana Saturn and Satan are pronounced the same. "To take the smallest step forward, even just to exist," says Cioran, "requires a minimum of villainy." Temper, Tempter. I keep trying to lose mine.

———————

Bede records the pun—*non Angli, sed Angeli*—the English are confused with angels. Rome founded where Saturn hid. We all get our promised land, eventually. Then break it. Small crops first, corn, tobacco. A GM Plant. I've heard we'll be out of lead by 2040, car batteries. I don't even see 2020. All this I say in passing. In passing Lordstown.

———————

Coleridge proposed an essay on puns. Freud started it. Freud's case histories read to me like fantastical New World accounts, the convincing mixture fact and fabrication, foretelling a land we need to believe exists partly to believe we do. For his faults, Freud's the Saturn of our age: castrated, deposed, by no means the end of the universe, but a good harsh starting point for the stare into chaos.

———————

Lips. Lisp. Slip. Nothing says more about us than our mouths.

———————

A *dual* in the individual. Sometimes I think I'm creating a monster. Homonculus I have called up from the nothingness to serve the village. But something's gone wrong. It sees more than it is supposed to. It reads labels in dumpsters. It hears triple. It tracks eavesdroppings. It roams the earth homelessly. Jester turned tester, it speaks my poems, swallows fire. It knows I can only take a few words, and it helps me pick and choose, pack them tight so I can unfold them later. It believes I will need this road.

———————

Cuyahoga River. Burning as it's freezing. I'm from a national punchline. What centuries of love poets only proposed, Cleveland made real. Twice, in fact—the first time the river caught fire no one remembers. That was before a television in every home and wise-cracking talk show hosts. The country breathes easier knowing Cleveland's there. There there. You'll forgive me if my style is somewhat off-hand. Call it the Cleveland Cavalier.

———————

Past the Kent exit, Tree City, U.S.A. *Tarmacadam* to *tarmac* is not the fall of Adam. It's the fall of something, something subtle, but we've hung enough on the tree for now. Function, says the Auditor, must stand up to form; weak puns don't work, a pun must smack us in at least two of our faces. One's state is one's taste, okay. Waldenbooks may sound like Buchenwalds, but they aren't.

———————

Cuyahoga again, "crooked river," remember. A brief glimpse of the Cleveland skyscrapers. Beyond that, Lake Erie, and Oliver Hazard Perry's famous line. *Ours* is such a funny little word. Like us, plural. But more like us, possessive.

———————

Macadamization. Devastation. Assimilation. An *-ation* word is from the principle part of a verb implying completed past action. A nation is "a having been born." I is an -ation.

GO TRIBE.

Strongsville tollbooth is the last I'll see. Almost home. At the junction of 82 and 71, the SHELL sign looks shorter than it used to. I was looking forward to seeing it. I remember it 200 feet high, lit up yellow with red block letters, always, it seemed, one letter flickering, an intermittent HELL. Or was it S ELL? It used to preside. Maybe the trees got taller. I used to imagine who with a .22 made it his job to shoot out that same proclamation at least biannually over my boyhood corner of the world.

With me as with Williams: difficult to get the news from poems. Difficult, but. "Make it new." "Go on your nerve." "Say it in American"—a century of button-sized injunctions. Take a violin, we learned, and strip it of all resemblance. Watch the news or the Cubists tonight? I fiddle while Rome is burning. I fiddle while Rome is burning Jerusalem.

Saturn. Decay and dissolution, especially before a period of rebirth. A lapse is not the Fall. Lapse makes leaps. A lapse is a sepal. Be fruitful, multiply. Who is how.

A Fête

We wanted to be succored
and we were suckered:
gobsmack over goblets,
toe-holds where finger
sandwiches should be,
the beer sophisticated,
the talk domestic. Beauty,
like death, you never know
who gets it. She gets it.
A belle, I'm told.
A beau, he's tied.
Sure, you can verb
(professor said) a noun
but not an adjective—
about which time
I blanked, the lights
shorted and a cow
in some proximity
lowed.

Nothing pressing tomorrow?
How about some pressing
tonight? Words were cheap,
and the least groped for.
Most, in the vernacular,
high. Wine came next
to felicitate conversation,
which it did: we ordered
white, all got red, all
got drinking stunk.

Some popped a cork
above the suds then
copped a pork below.
We wanted to be fêted
and we were fetid: souls
so gleefully at odds as most
would be at peace. Minds
in oneness this year,
next year in Tunis.

A French Statue

FOR MOTHER

Liberty's so high up, you think—you expected her
down-to-earth. No such luck, you clasp
at your mother's skirt. She knows this place
where names get changed, some by accident,

some not, where immigrants learn a new *sur-*,
or as you'll see here, a *last*. You're next. Your
name. Your next of kin. *Next,* you'll learn,
is how to move lines (not queues) no matter what

that kind Irish passenger taught you. *Next,*
please. Next. And this the city you heard of but
a year ago as your parents explained in Hungarian.
Soon enough you'll be in school, they'll ask

what you speak and *Magyar,* you'll repeat,
Mud-your—a tongue pronounced with mud.
Hungary you'll learn for its own pun by first
Thanksgiving. Turkey you will learn to stuff.

More and more each year, you'll grow
to love the Salvation Army Santa ringing bells
to bring Christmas. You'll give me coins to feed
his kettle and say these people were your first

taste of America, sugar cookies, weak cocoa,
Willkommen, what the lady said to you—so
strangely, with a *will*—those first few crumbs
of welcome, have some, *Or is it "Bienvenue"?*

Neither, thank you. You're welcome now.
Hard to tell you from a local. Hard to tell you, too,
what I've clung to, phrases you fed, American as
mom and apple pie. Brand spanking new. Chew

the fat. Take a load off. Each a measure of freedom:
the Drinking Gourd, forty acres and a mule, a chicken
in every pot, a man on the moon; and odd numerologies
of urgency: second wind, the fourth quarter, the bottom of

the ninth. At contradictions we never stopped: free
rein, Statue of Liberty; you had me take it all with
displaced patience, just in case, any way the wind blows,
you never know. In the meantime, make *yourself*

at home. All systems go.

Media

Meat comes from
the supermarket, news
from the TV. Or wait—
do we have the order
straight? Does *media*
begin with *meaty*?
Are stories hung
on hooks, inspected,
sliced and wrapped
in plastic, selected,
served at dinner
or as a late-night
snack? Are problems
beefs? Is turkey
talked? Questions
ducked? Answers
left-wing, right-wing,
chicken? Is the anchorman
a ham? The camera—
does it add ten
pounds? It polices
pigs. It freezes
breasts. It carves
the thigh. It roasts
our rumps. It meats
the eye.

Toes

A decent docent doesn't forget the Cleveland Thinker,
Rodin's bronze cast of 1880, deconstructed in 1970

by a protest bomb that blew his little green feet off.
As statements go, you'd be saying a lot to target

the Western man in thought—but the news exploded,
cameras flashed, and no one quite could figure out why.

Why so low? After all, he's the Thinker: might as well knock
his cogitating block off, or that guilty accomplice wrist

taking on his grave weight. It's misguided—isn't it?—
to strike so far below the belt, at such innocent bystanders

as toes, where the toes position themselves, as far
from human thought as thought humanly possible.

But Cleveland's weekend anarchists weren't fools:
they knew too well the complicity of toes; that rotting

underclass, the corny boasts of balance, first in battle
and bathtubs, ambassadors of dance, best propaganda

forward. They hold little thinkers back. Take that, Big T,
your two thug bigtoes too, and those eight little capitalist

piggies you trot around. Us, us, us, and the market—
that's all you think about. We, we, we, all the way home.

It Has an I

History has to live with what was here,
has to whitewash, revise til worthy. Ah,
history: whole Hittite wharves awash,
whole throwaway vistas, this hit here,
that hit there, a slavish Yore. Wow, wish
I was there. Worth a visit. Who they lash,
how she rots, why Hiawatha, trite lives
that ravish awhile, those wise worthy
hysterias. Whatever. A Shiloh with two
harsh vowels—*i, o*—that shy wit, we hear it.
History's lavish three—what *I?* what *owe?*
why?—are short. It is a heath with wolves.
How it thrashes alive with awry. Those
who wish, starve. Oh why? It has a letter I.

Feet

Recalling the Standing Fishes Bible, an 1806 edition in which Ezekiel 47:10 reads "And it shall come to pass that the fishes shall stand upon it" instead of "fishers"

Sticky, floundering, floppy, numerous:
once I helped birth a litter of puppies.
Every scrawny dog checked out—two eyes,
two ears, one tail—except the runt who came
with his paws on backward, pads up. Whining
every step, high-register misunderstandings.
The farmer, pious man, wouldn't hear of this,
held him down in a tub til no bubbles.

But some of the new ideas do all right.
Now and then there's a two-headed cow to pull out,
or a tongueless frog to dissect, each destined
for little: their share of the pain prepared them.
Always a chick with no beak who can't break
the first layer. Always more loose talk among fish
about feet. Flukes are older than you
can imagine; the whale wasn't one picked to make it.

Diet Meats

I like drama eaten in.
Lake air. I need a mint.
I like a dinner, a tame

Ariel diet, a.k.a., in men.
I like a dent, a marine
mania. I drink eel tea,

mandarin tea, i.e., like
karate, a lime, dine-in
linen. I take Madeira.

Make it adrenaline. I,
real Medea, I, anti-kin:
alienate me. I drink a

martini. A keen Delia
(I mean Ideal). Ink tear
in a tinker. A made-lie

in a limeade. In a trek,
a dreamlike tie-in, an
entrée. I'm Kali. Naiad

(I mean Diana) reel kit.
Like in Ariadne. Mate
like a tread-in (I mean

meat) inner Aïda, like
a like. (I mean trade-in.)
I like a maiden rent, a

Lear kinda matinee. (I
mean real kinda.) I tie
inner kite, I, dame à la

Iliad. Tie an arm, knee.
Tie ankle. I marinade
And I eat men like air.

Court Seated

If facts don't fit,
we say the story
doesn't hold water.

Law is all awash, aloof
when testimony is measured
by liquid, alcohol

by proof. What do we say
when we say, "wine
is truth"? Is justice blind

drunk? Enough to make us
puke? Judges,
reputed for sobriety,

will still occasionally
order in the quart.
Lawyers pass the bar

each day, with whom?
the bottle or the bailiff?
So *that's* why we sit

when called to the stand.
Raise your right hand.
Take the fifth.

Time

I. VIRGINIA IS FOR LOVERS

The license plate on my life read CA VA,
transplanted from California, keen on the way
the French don't change a syllable (*Ça va? Ça va*)
to say, "How goes it?" and answer that "It goes."
You don't change a letter. You change your tone.
I left what people leave in San Francisco. Hearts
grow back, tongues return, something takes the place
of person, place, and thing—some great pronoun
(my word). I was enamored of it. It drove those
foolish days together, it drove at least that license
plate. It conquered all. It was somewhere that couldn't
be split. It was all I needed to compose myself, it stood
for love or place or time. Like black, it went with
everything. Like with everything, it went black.

II. NEW DOMINION BOOKSHOP, CHARLOTTESVILLE

which, every so often, would show me the Old.
Renaissance mendicants milled in from the mall, made
straight for Shakespeare—I kid you not—or the local
gentleman poet strolled in, or a matron would scold
her misbehaving granddaughter: *Nawt vera ledalike.*
But the days of the Leda, like, lady, were over: the girl
was evidence. Bored in baseball cleats as grandma combed
cookbooks, no belle-of-the-ball, no belle-of-the-ballpark;
her stance said, *I'll swat any Swain or Swann who dares
come up with a change-up. Or a come-on.* Her job
was to put the gods in their place, as I did each night,
scribbling these entries at a lull, shuffling mislaid myths
back into Classics, or else, Religion. The rest
the next shift could sort. What didn't fit was History.

III. TIMES DISPATCH, RICHMOND

You have to understand, I come from *Plain Dealers*.
Which is why this is all news to me, the *Mid Virginia*
Trading Post, the *Old Town Crier*, the *Daily Progress*.
Stein said you could name a few American states
and the words start to sound like poetry. I guess.
But for me, it's these, *Old Bridge Observer*,
Northern Neck Tide, unwieldy or deliberately outmoded,
The Weekly Telegraph, *Virginian-Pilot* and *Ledger Star*,
with occasional bursts of nostalgia, *National Coal Leader*,
or the blunt-and-loving-it, *Bull Mountain*.
Sure, we blamed them—the *Independent Messenger*,
Bland Messenger, the *Weekly Messenger Classified*—
but still we stacked, bundled, and bore them among us.
Times Mirror, *Times Register*, *Times Dispatch*.

IV. FOUR, IVY

The Tops. Quartets. Horsemen of the Apocalypse.
The Marks of the Church. The Corners of the Earth.
The Oceans. Roosevelt's Four Freedoms: two ofs
and two froms. A reason in July for fireworks.
The ineffable tetragrammaton. The effable four-letter
words, all immersed in sex and excrement. The broken
four-minute mile. The many stabs they honestly took
at Fourierism, a utopian social unit 1,600 souls across,
a perfect square, each square a digit of the body
politic. Fourierists worked four-sided plots,
their most menial tasks were the best rewarded. O
for simpler days, when we lived in tune with the seasons.
Given world enough and time, surely we could make
a Fourth World of it. We have the dimensions.

V. LIBRARY, ALEXANDRIA

It's insult to injury, obscenity to obsolescence,
taking call numbers off a computer screen
and jotting them on the backs of scrap catalog cards.
Check this out: pens are reading books by their covers,
spines require a demagnetizing swipe before they're yours
(or else, alarms). Not the library I grew up on, but
it might as well be anywhere's. Paper culture worried
Wordsworth, "shrines so frail" for all the effort.
If we sleep better than the Romantics, we have silicon
to thank: our sand against the hourglass,
our universe wired and webbed in a Blakeian grain.
Brave New World is out, but can be here in
two days from one of our branches.
Life in Greece and Rome? That we can have in a day.

VI. CORRESPONDENCE, NATURAL BRIDGE

What I remember were his initials carved in stone
twenty feet off the creek, father of the country, look,
he signed for it. Back in Charlottesville, I worked for
the Washington Papers, a second job at grad-student wages,
squinting into microfiche at the elegant cursives of
a hundred dead, decorous hands. George's strokes
were gracious, calm, not without quirks—a casual small *w*
which passed for an *n* ("My Fellon Citizens," I smirked).
Why not make up the past?—they made it up as they went.
Among historians I was the sham, misleading and misled
as a Spring forgery. The mistake fakes make is how
hands change: the edgy early years; an older flow;
a forger is many men well, to be even one. George
revised. First-hand another lie most cannot tell.

VII. GRAY, GREYS POINT

Gray with an *a, grey* with an *e*? *Grey* with an *e*
looks greyer. To me. But pity a man like Caxton,
1490, the final word on spelling, if extant, unheeded,
as in his preface to an English *Aeneid,* where a word
like "book" could be spelled three ways and all on the very
same page! French had invaded everything, the oldest
stuff read like German. What's an earnest Anglicist
to do—no reference, no referee—how does one write
the simplest things? Time was, eggs were over easy.
Time was, things were black and white. And in such
golden ages as when tongues were rolled into one,
an emperor wished all Rome had a single neck.
Grey with an *e* for me, but long live the other guy,
the guide in the dark who can't tell Virgil from Vergil.

VIII. PRONUNCIATION, DANTE

No, not to hell and back again, here it rhymes
with *quaint.* So don't bother abandoning anything,
ye who enter here, it's only spoken as *paint,* or *taint,*
or as if deception crept up slow, a hiss, an air
(or lack thereof) to play canaries dead asleep.
A *faint,* or *feint.* Say it's coal alone that guides you,
not salvation, no audience with the multifoliate rose;
just duty, fuel duty, the dust's *Same old, same old*
at your throat, carbide mush on the coat you wore in,
or your neighbor's coat the day he was pinned
and pronounced—what was it now?—*dead*—
then you might not put much stock in pronunciation.
Or *saint.* You may find deep down a place you
don't believe in, cavern that won't echo. Or *cain't.*

IX. SOLDIERS, APPOMATTOX

They do a fine job at the Court House, walking the line
between those who heard of the Civil War in school
and those who learned the War of Northern Aggression.
Perennial gentleman, Lee thought to surrender his saber,
but the mud-spattered, uncomely victor waved him off.
Archilochos would've liked Grant: *I don't go for generals who*
tower over troops, lordly elegant with locks, neat beards.
He liked a stumpy grunt, flagrantly bowlegged,
rocksteady on his feet and in his core, enormous.
And Grant might've cared for the fragments—*Fields fattened*
by corpses—I suspect that'd be the extent of any
mutual admiration. Permission to speak freely. Denied.
Permission to drop shield and save skin. Denied.
Permission to drum and dutifully die. Granted. Fall in.

X. DECIMATION, TENTH LEGION

ROMAN CAN   DESOLATE ROBUST SKIES   HOOT OF   F
UNERAL OWLS   HOT IN GLOW   IGNOBLENESS   NOW
TENSE   O GO JULY FORTH   ONE WIT EVERY   THIN
SHADOWING   ARES IMAGE IN THEIR REAR   DINGBAT
RIGHT   DARKLING BLING   OUR OL LEGIONS HAVENT
EASED EVER   AVE THEY   MATER ROMANA   AVE
THEM   JUTTING   LESS THINKING   O ERRANT ING
LES   TONGUE   TODAY   TIME   UNSTREAMS   VERA
CITY   O ANUS FACED USA   STOP PLYING   WITH
FREEDOM   GOT URNS   ASHES O ASHES   AS TOYS
MEN DIE   WHAT IS THE USE OF FIRE   RUSTIEST
AMOR   LUST OF OLD   RED O   RAGE   OH SO UNDULY
JETSAM LED   THAT'S A RAP   WAY   TO FARE   OUT
FARING   UNDEFEATED MONTH   WITH   NO   IDES

XI. MENSURA, POUND

The biting medieval air of our writing programs might
appeal to him, rote copying of texts, young scribes
adapting elders' drafts. It's the god remade of meter that
Pound would chuck *The Cantos* at: *With mensura*
hath no man any sturdier house of cards, measureth
no craftsman his iambs against his judgment, lines
not to witness only corroborate, and verse made to scan
and sell quickly. WITH MENSURA lines grow predictable
the tone-deaf think to sing with mensura, mensura blunteth
the blunt with a cudgel a dull one, Jackson Pollock came not
by mensura, nor Kandinsky. Mensura trusteth the chiseller,
mensura inspires odes to the obvious, Mensura
CONTRA SATURAM They have bought dead feet new shoes
Corpses are set to music at the behest of mensura. . . .

XII. EXPOSED, JAMESTOWN

You notice it once, once like never before, and then
you notice it everywhere, it's made that critical wrinkle
in your brain and now the wrinkle won't iron out
no matter how you press and steam. Back again
in commercials for, of all things, antiperspirant—
"Never let them see you sweat"—the embarrassing
reek and groan of exposed weakness. In Jamestown,
the militia drilled where the natives wouldn't witness,
for if they See your Learners miss what they aim at
they will think the Weapon not so terrible. That's what
I read, and now it's everywhere, behind closed doors,
in barriered restroom stalls, this fear of being caught,
wrinkle-frees around our knees, the pubic suddenly
public, all eyes on us. We're sweating bullets.

XIII. CREDIT, CHECK

In a world of what and who you know, *thyself*
is not a very lucrative answer. Thus, résumé.
Thus, CV. Thus reference and recommendation,
thus glowing blurbs on an otherwise banal book.
Oh, those high school English honors every year
are little help here, at my unremarkable job,
and Latin, the oldest, most stolen office supply,
rusts in my ROM while I RAM through another day.
Here credit spawns belief—it's backward etymology—
my work and *my work* on different shifts, drifting job
to job. And poetry, like any hard boss, upbraids me,
suspects me of moonlighting and strings me along
with praise not pay. Good work tonight.
You're a credit to this organization.

XIV. DUBIOUS, WATER VIEW

We're mostly made of water, study shows,
and true to a point, depending how you lower
your microscope. We'll try to go a little deeper
here, we'll stop at nothing. By now you know
there's less to us than we even dreamed, the matter
any one of us musters wouldn't fill this period.
Being mostly what we aren't already, that's
good news—we're underway—takes the pressure off
oblivion's big shoes. We think we're really something,
and we are, something of a blip to the Nothing Cycle,
but take the water view if you want its opinion.
It's nice out there in the waves, under the stars,
a trusty set of coordinates, where place, like almost
nothing else, bobs in its minutes and seconds.

XV. ANOTHER, CLEVELAND

What are we, but what we mistake ourselves for?
The brashest fact of my childhood—was I five?—
learning there were other Kevins. Might have said seven
for the rhyme, but you'd probably think I was slow
("Second grade, the lad hadn't grasped that?") and
good thing too, since you're counting, I wasn't named
Nate, the temptation would be too (don't say it)
powerful. Do you even believe a syllable of this?
This life is a living remembered over a shoulder:
breadcrumb trail remapped into meaning years after
from crowshit cairns which pigs mistake for truffles.
Three days in your life that no art will recapture:
the day you were born, the day death sank in deep,
and the day you divined you weren't so damn special.

XVI. CAMPFIRE, LIGNUM

The world shone in letters, Lucretius believed:
in firewood (*lignis*) was hidden (*ignis*) fire. Whatever
kindles your tinder. His *mater* flirted with matter
for that matter. Linguistics, logistics—two sticks
perhaps one shouldn't rub together—but if,
on a night like this, by firelight and stars, one hears
the *pater* in the local patter, whose pattern
would that be? Father time, mother tongue,
we will be true to you in our fashion:
our fashion is to read what we choose to read.
A possible good in the bonfire—not the bone—
faint flag in the conflagration—not the blaze.
All things are fire, flame's said to have tongues,
our dignity and ignorance, our signatures.

XVII. MODE, EDOM

In another realm, but obviously not here,
the haves need only shave, the have-nots
have tons. Give us this day our daily beard,
they pray. There, Kevins shine like knives.
In anagrams, a man's grain: but that alone won't
cut it. Time is the item. Minglers are gremlins,
no ideas but aside, no nights but in things,
there are miracles, yes, and there are claimers.
This mode is a demo, so when near the dome of Edom,
start at the Mansion of Onanism, walk down
Tester Street, turn at the corner of Seneca and Seance:
Delight is the place you're looking for (it's lighted).
Over this town, God casts his slipper, his ripples.
Look to the sky: there's choosing in *hoc signo.*

XVIII. ROOM, OTTOMAN

Do you suppose the great kings of Ur would care
their legacy lives on the lips of men, if only a prefix
for the pretentious—ur-this, ur-that—or do you guess
the Ming Dynasty is ennobled by these eponymous
take-out boxes and chopsticks littering the furniture,
TV alert to the pious Mayan custom of burying relatives
beneath the dwelling floor, a fact we find more than a little
disturbing, practiced today by society's least desirables.
Reconcile that. Reconcile that to the next image up,
goosestepping troops—uber-this, uber-that—fragments
of empires loose in the lounge of language, our to-die-for
living room, fake persian rug, dusty venetians, the feudal
(nearly futile) displays, or how we've made a crude table
of what we know not long ago was fit for feet alone.

XIX. HONEYMOON, WARM SPRINGS

Late fall, a century not yet into its teens,
we have slipped one honeymoon afternoon
into the thermo-mother. Water meets our body heat,
unaware of its degrees. Only we have degrees.
We study anthropometry: tree-limb, foothill, the hand
of God near enough, whether or not He will show it.
Our days-new rings would corrode in this stew;
they stayed in our pockets, in the changing room.
We love. We hate what's afoot, what's at hand, a base-
ten band—commandments, percentages, centuries.
America too has made its vows: it won't give up
an inch it don't have to. A world in arms, our trip's
last leg. We recall, among the imperial conversions,
fahrenheit is submerged "experience."

XX. NAMES, APPALACHIA

Most scenery is lost on me. Names mean
everything. You could say these mountains
blink back words like dust motes. Words
won't bring one down, maybe water, given time.
Given time, the right word might. The right word
in the right hand, curled like a plan in a foreman's
clenched fist, the way we have of mining
these days, not veining out at depths and at risk
but shrewdly chopping the mountains down.
Don't be so certain the noun is dead. These days.
Don't be so sure the imperishable world
is, and the letters only stand-ins. Whatever's called
may be called up, called out, called back. In time.
These mountains are still appellations.

No-Fat Ice

Sure you think of ants. And sucking marrow. But what one rarely
hears about are the pages of neologisms he thought fit just for
kindling—*Quesper: a Whisper'd Question . . . Masturbaton: excessive
Hyperbaton, putting the inner Heart before the Intercourse*—his
friends at his trashcan really lapping it up ("This stuff is genius!")
and Thoreau breathing beleaguered heat into his hands and
muttering, *Time to start the beans.* Who knows what he really
wanted. He was one of those always telling fat people how they were
going to die sooner, why not the Walden Diet?—there may be a book
in it—do you like that title? Everything has to pull its own weight.
Even these schmucks trucking ice frigid mornings off to India, light
between the trees like a guru who sees through you, Thoreau slowly
shaking his head at their snowball misses—*Slimify, slimify*—and
sipping centuries ahead of himself on the prototype tofu shake.
Biting on ice cubes—the soul has a weight—just make the time. The
beans do, like beyond was their job, what two of us so industrious!
He thought he invented the trick of burning a long log in the middle.
If he knew his cholesterol, he'd have been intolerable. But today's
eternal present is over, the heavies and their thermoses long gone,
the sun has broken its egg on the horizon. Thoreau at a bean-wax
candle, scratches away with his nib and twists his nighttime sports
into tomorrow's tinder. The massive men, the mass of men—what
difference? The only journal he wrote for was his. Any warmth you
could get from that flame would be too little. *Diet quesperation,* he
scrabbles on a scrap, hating it before the ink is even dry.

At Rushmore

A man crouches low to fool history or distance,
camera adjusting for his special shot, a wife's
smiling head eclipsing Roosevelt. The strange
resulting administration. Surrounding gawkers
get the picture, and one sham past is snapped
after another. After another. And this young son
of the country, he's got ice cream on his mind.
His parents stare up, but he's more enthralled
with what may slip any minute: Rocky Road,
an industrious tongue. And what's on
everyone else's? The syllables *rush* and *more*
have brought us this far, true tourists some,
most foreign in our own country. Seeing
comes first, brochures next, the legendary
boasts of need-to-know (that the peak
was named for a title inspector; that its sculptor
believed in big; that granite set a precedent,
intrusion). Wherever from, the unforeseen
quirks of production intrigue: having to change
the plan to match the mountain's emerging vision,
moving the visage of Jefferson to Washington's
other shoulder (his second face, the one in place
today) or striking the ominous vein of lead
which penetrates Lincoln's head. In these,
this mountain seems to have known, carved
its people even. Near the base, rubble remains—
a talus of blasted stones, dropped names—
the part of the image we may come closest to.

The Faucet

The sink is costing me precious
concentration. *Poet   poet   poet*
it mocks, mating call for a plumber.
My friends suggest I should write more
toward the impossible, around the unreal.
I tell them my theme's America,
what's the diff? Water's expensive
and money's supposed to trickle,
the national pastime's a diamond
made of dirt. It's difficult *not*
to write satire, an old spout spurted.
He's right: bills pop up, sense flies out,
a pitcher's catching the faucet's fluent
language. I myself don't spicket.

———————

The plumber does, thank God,
know his pipes. Chit-chatting a little,
we try to jive our slippery jargons.
"Long as you're here, could you snake
the commode?" I ask (with a blue-collar
coyness—I might've called it "the throne").
By accent, I'd trace this plumber to Pittsburgh—
the way he says "toilet" (*twirl-it*), the way
he says "faucet" (*force-it*). He asks what I do
(my skin crawls) and I tell him, saying poetry's

like his business: if the job's done right,
you never need see the pipes—just know
they're flowing. His look says I'm full
of shit. *Twirl it,* I think, *don't force it.*

Die Satan!

Go easy on the Prince of Darkness, please.
Guy got a bad rap; everyone pinning
personal worsts on him, passing their bucks
back to Beelzebub. Yes, it's true,
the dog ate my family, or asked me to,
some record in reverse made me do it.
(The Stones alone show him sympathy,
the Grateful Dead call him friend.)
Whenever my idle hands need work,
I like to play the advocate. His aliases
fill phonebooks full, and the numbers
are rarely as easy as 666. Open anywhere,
let your fingers do the walking—
Old Scratch to what but our old itch.

It's Smut

Sweet. Thin. I know, i.e., I
knew. Twenties. I—oh I—I
stew. I hint ewe. I oink-
oink: "Hi, sweetie." Twin
Teens II. Wowie. Kith 'n
Kin. To wet his wienie,
teenie with no kiwis,
we (I-we) tie hot skin in.
I knot, we tie. I win, she
whinnies, to wit. I eke:
"I won't." I seethe, I wink.
Two swine. I eek! I hint,
sweetie, I know I hint.
I know it when I see it.

Ears

*Recalling the Ears to Ear Bible, an edition of 1810 in which
Matthew 13:43 reads "Who hath ears to ear, let him hear"*

Words fail, wisdom holds, and I agree
but they do it beautifully. I'm fishing
with a friend from East Tennessee—
Deep Tennessay, he corrects, I quote,
as we're holding shallow to shore.
(I should add this friend isn't really
there. He winks.) Taking my glasses off
their ears, the sunset world goes orangely
Impressionistic. Calls to mind a theory:
Cézanne, Monet, was it talent or mere
near-sightedness? This is where and when
it's good to have no friend, the times
when art seems the art of going blind
by deaf, words through water, all
appears mishearing. *Whatever you lack,*
says my friend, drawling *like* distinctly,
an answer perhaps twice right, whatever
we lack, we like. Today, it's not just ears
failing well, it's the bait, it's the light.
Fish seem happier for it, so does
the night, coming on, but not before
my boatmate cracks the last impossible
beer, clunks it (aluminum's clink) against
mine and says, *Ain't this the LAUGH?*
Life, I grasp, though it takes me
a second. It throws us both back.

Hate

Recalling the Lions Bible, an 1804 edition in which 1 Kings 8:19 reads "But thy son that shall come forth out of thy lions" instead of "loins"

Empires are my premise, Archilochos my schoolchair.

More was my first word and that means Rome.

Denotation is detonation, be careful. As car fuel:

at home in the anger, at home on the range.

Does the den exist to justify the manes?

I must mean amens. I must name names:

I hate that there's an Amherst in man's heart.

I hate that there's a Hitler in the lair. If you

can't feel the heat, there's reason (there's no sear).

Look outside (tedious) look inside (sin, die).

Satire, as rite. Rage is my gear. These

images only I-games? So be it—rather

throw notes than stone, draw words not sword.

The insulted despise the insulated, and burn for lack

of a letter. Hate is the heat. Hate, the *a*.

A Tone Deficit

Can't tell your *oh* from your *ah*? Go, go or else
go ga-ga. What, were you born in a barn? Oh.
Ah. What do you say when the dentist asks?
No novacaine? Nah. Then joke's on us, Jack:

we gnaw ourselves when we really ought to know.
Can't tell the force from the farce, nor our
cores from our cars. The horde works hard in this
new nation of shopkeeps, moles in malls, minding

our stores when we should be minding our stars.
Harmony, whoremoney—can we even tell
the showman from the shaman? Or are we
the worst kind of tourists, doing La France

in low fronts, in shorts at Chartres and so
alone in our *élan*? Nope. We're Napoleons
of nowhere, hopeless going on hapless,
unable to tell our Elbas from our elbows.

To the African Muse

'Twas mercy brought me from my Pagan land,
my pagan rags, my howl. Abduct me. Rent from
home, fed not many crumbs, warm gag, partly
negro woman, partly bed-charm — my fat gums.
Damn far. 'Twas clergyman bought me. My pro
a con. Straw for bed. Ample rum. My myth gang-
mercy, my motto gang-rape. Draw numb flash
from memory: bland, gaunt gasp. What mercy?

Idea

Was it
rolled out
or tabled?
Couldn't tell
which end
was up,
what odds
told treasure
from trash.
I recall
(vaguely recalling)

we threw
one out
(idea / a die)
but again
that but
reminded me
each first
is loaded
either way,
there is
at last

no last.
Thought we
broke the
bank and
mold when
that one

turned up;
of course
it meant
that two
was cast.

Test of Merit

Our cares are non-mighty I utter theirs are real.
Our anthems are coy ring trite theirs are a rule.
Our hymns are ocean-grit errata theirs lie true.
Our sutra gem-rare their chants are elite irony.
Our charm attires are tiny are gone theirs lure.
Our terms irritate theirs are Herculean agony.
Our interiors are change theirs rarely mutate.
Our nothings are eerie tar theirs ultra creamy.
Our tears are thorny urine theirs relate magic.
Our games are corny hint theirs are true retail.
Our canyon a rash rut theirs e'er err legitimate.
Our grins are arch yet no theirs laureate merit.
Our true achings are Troy-men their era is later.
Our chains are grey theirs turn Rome retaliate.
Our canons are grim they lie theirs are true art.
Our myths are ignorance, theirs are literature.

Data

Given givens,
one's got lots
to go on, lots
to prove. One
watches watches,
figures figures,
one thinks one knows
one lives. Goofs
and guesses later,
any given notetaker
nervously addresses
next:
who gave or else
what gives?

Astute Chinese Aside

Lao Tsu and Confucius met once in the city. To have been a fly on
the wall for that conversation! Confucius would treat the virtuous
well, the bad badly; Lao Tsu treated all living souls the same.
Confucius thought a poor and filial scholar is best. His host cared
little for bookishness. The self-restrained, Confucius would go on,
seldom would go off. To Lao Tsu the river knew where it was headed.
The tea got tepid and little was said. Then the Old Sage sighed that
everything, even that fly on the wall, is one ten-thousandth of the
mystery. And Confucius nodded and swatted it.

Denuded, deluded, who knows what human nature is? A dull feeling
that it's all near-miss — the Great Wall to the Great Mall; the inner-
life to the sinner-life; *ben-xing, ren-xing* — or as it was mentioned
in Mencius: *Ox Mountain was covered by trees, but it stands near
a populous city. Came axes, came saws, came cattle, came sheep . . .
and people who see it today think it always was treeless.* Denuded by
drives, deluded by droves, who dead or alive may spell what human
nature is?

Ez sez find a new Greece in China. You have your orders — Ez sez.
Obstructive! Obtuse! Obstruse! Before those stony villages named
for saints, before the saints, before the Athenian schemer of *The
Republic,* hermits of that land would feed on ferns before taking one
grain gathered under corruption. Name a Beat poet untaxable as

that! I spent his century's final ticks digging for it in San Francisco, kept every pithy paper slip those dim-sum diners gave me, hoping— what?—wisdom entered from the belly? *Your ability to find the silly in the serious will take you far.* So far, so good . . . but still so far, so far. Everywhere, men with crumbs and cookies with fortunes.

Authentic

The land was ours before we were the land's,
Frost wrote. Slander. Was he blue? He weaned
a werewolf, breast-held us. He answered not
to snare but defend where we are: owl-slash
at wee hours, flea on web strands. We're held
on a lens, deeds of war, there's the Law. We rub
wet brow and see ourself as her, we, the land.
Rawness. He enfolded war lore, but see what
he released? The land wasn't ours. We few rob-
bed the land (raw steel). We saw our shore, fen,
forests bleed. Heal. We were our wants. Hand
the wolf new bread, sure he eats. Words lean.
Words turn foe. Were we the lash-laden, base
new beast of nature? ladderless? where? who?
when? artless? No. Refuse. We dared howl, beat
far on westward, see blue. We had her, stolen.

Meta-Forest

Every summer for eight years came my job
superimposing the known on the unknown.
Northeastern Ohio forest before us,
college kid, camp counselor, I'd pick a sprig
of pine, spread its and my five fingers:
W-H-I-T-E. "White pine," I showed
my campers, "you know by the letters."
To get it, they had to be able to spell,
and usually could, age twelve. Exceptions
I'd teach by the palms of their hands,
known on unknown, hands-on nature,
palms upturned, see, white no matter what.

———

Which brought us to sassafras.
They liked the sound of that, the *sass*.
It was memorable: four kinds of leaves,
half of which look like misfit mittens.
Right thumb. Left thumb. Two thumbs.
No-thumb-at-all. "Plus, it tastes good,"
I'd demonstrate, pick off a new stem,
chew, wait. "Ew . . . bitter,"
some young initiates would spit.
"Hold on," I said. Then aftertaste.

———

Red pine, *R-E-D,* back to the sprigs.
I'd take one down. Show three. Then
why was this bewildering? Why
did it all seem backward? Words
we learned early. Earth's characters
oddly next, like this, like that, a retrofit.

What we knew we knew by the letters.

———————

We knew by the rhymes:
Leaves of three, leave it be.
Eyes to the side, often hide.
And not just rhymes: a beat
a kid could take to college,
Beer before liquor, et cetera,
same tricks he was taught, then
taught. We'd even weave
down a creek bed looking for animals.
"First one to find one gets to lead."
The smart-ass always presented,.
as animal, himself. "Cheating!"
the rest of them usually screamed.
Of course it was. "He leads."

———————

"Eyes in front," I purposefully observed,
someone having found a frog.
"Often hunt!" they yelled in captive unison

(quick answers, I hinted, would make the hike
go faster). "Hunt with what?" I posed
and paused, so poised and so socratic.

Smart ones platoed along, "Their tongue."

———————

Tongues, eyes, hands,
everything about the forest
echoed, everything meant. Me? I carried
letters in my head, a head or so above theirs,
rescheming the ancient lines:
O from the eye, *K* from the palm of the hand,
OK, OK, eye-hand coordination. We broke
for water, let the stragglers catch up.

———————

Mmmm.
Cold water
over the wrists.
The mind
persists:
M from waves
of water,
K from the cup
of my hand.
KM, KM
against my lips,
initials of

ablution.
KM, KM,
cool slaps
in the face.
A name
that won't slip
my fingers.

———————

KM, take a letter: no sass, no aftertaste,
no aleph as a breather. And answer this:
was it better back in the wilderness, better
back in the ideograms? Fishing letters
from streams, *O*s from wild eyes, knowing *K*s
like the front of your hand? The land
an infinite alphabet, the river running
its anagram? Every time we paused
at an undisclosed pine, the letters grew
nomad-haggard to me: storm-blasted,
scaled down, packed light.

———————

And who could keep up with them?
One kid, winded, asked me the difference
between two words I kept using:
which steeper, *ravine* or *gully*?
"One has a *V,* one has a *U,*"
I told him, "how does *V* sound?"

"Like straight up and down."
"Right," I said. "And *U*?"

———————

Of course, I made that up. What's known
thrown on the whatnot (*known* in small letters,
letters in smaller letters, all standing
for standing, meaning once-removed
and hard to recapture)—maybe it helped
the hike go faster. Then always the crew
grew anxious, started to kick, throw sticks,
ask, when they'd gotten tired of the show,
"*Now* can we go back?"
OK, I'd think.

And the answer was no.

Notes

I.e.
A number of the poems in this collection are produced by anagrammatical method, each line being reconstructed letter by letter from the borrowed line in the poem. The borrowed line in this poem is from "Canto CXVI" by Ezra Pound.

Meditate Sea to Sea
The borrowed line is from "Let America Be America Again" by Langston Hughes.

It's a Cue, the Name
Line from "America" by Allen Ginsberg.

Famed Cities, section X; cf. Time, section X
The section titled "Dread, Phalanx" undergoes a decimation (every tenth letter of the poem is removed) and may be read after the letters have been removed in a poem of the "Time" sequence: "Decimation, Tenth Legion."

It's Tarmac
The following books were "in the trunk" as this piece was recorded: Cioran, E. M., *History and Utopia,* University of Chicago Press, 1998; Chevallier, Raymond, *Roman Roads,* Batsford, 1989; Culler, Jonathan (ed.), *On Puns: The Foundation of Letters,* Blackwell, 1988; Freud, Sigmund, *Jokes and Their Relation to the Subconscious,* 1905; Kennedy, Roger G., *Hidden Cities,* Free Press, 1994; Kostof, Spiro, *The City Shaped,* Bulfinch Press, 1994; McAdam, John Loudon, *A Practical*

Essay on the Scientific Repair and Preservation of Roads, 1819; Redfern, Walter, *Puns,* Blackwell, 1984; Schwartz, Regina M., *The Curse of Cain,* University of Chicago Press, 1997.

It Has an I
Line from "History" by Robert Lowell.

Diet Meats
Line from "Lady Lazarus" by Sylvia Plath.

It's Smut
Line from Justice Potter Stewart, his famous definition as given in a 1964 pornography decision.

To the African Muse
Line from "On Being Brought from Africa to America" by Phillis Wheatley.

Test of Merit
Line from "White Magic" by Derek Walcott.

Authentic
Line from "The Gift Outright" by Robert Frost.

BOOKS IN THE SERIES

The History of Anonymity
Jennifer Chang

Hardscrabble
Kevin McFadden

Field Folly Snow
Cecily Parks

Boy
Patrick Phillips